Dash Diet Cookbook For Beginners

A 28 days meal plan with many Mediterranean recipes that will help you keep under control diabetes, blood pressure, renal health and will assist you in weight loss

---

[Jennifer Green]

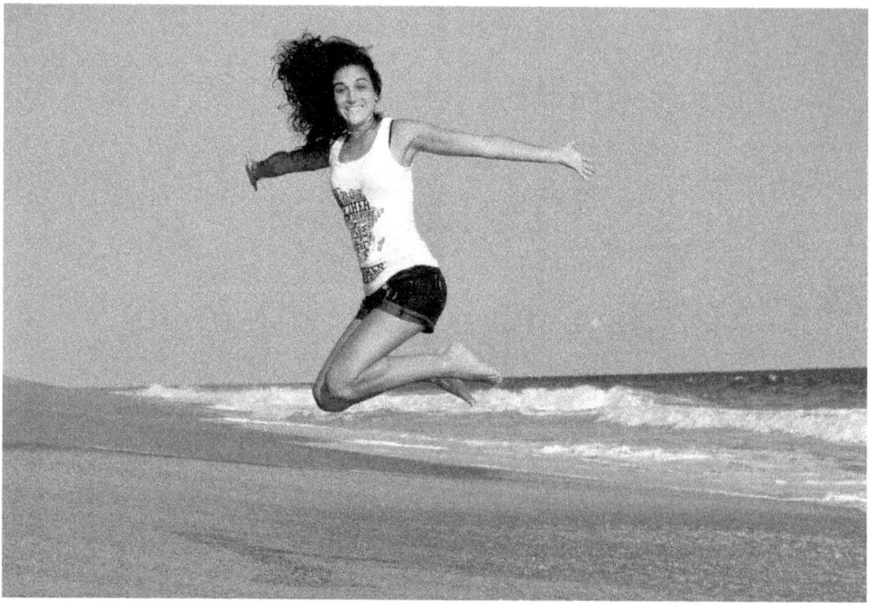

Text Copyright © [Jennifer Green]

All rights reserved. No part of this guide may be reproduced in any form without permission in writing from the publisher except in the case of brief quotations embodied in critical articles or reviews.

Legal & Disclaimer

The information contained in this book and its contents is not designed to replace or take the place of any form of medical or professional advice; and is not meant to replace the need for independent medical, financial, legal or other professional advice or services, as may be required. The content and information in this book has been provided for educational and entertainment purposes only.

The content and information contained in this book has been compiled from sources deemed reliable, and it is accurate to the best of the Author's knowledge, information and belief. However, the Author cannot guarantee its accuracy and validity and cannot be held liable for any errors and/or omissions. Further, changes are periodically made to this book as and when needed. Where appropriate and/or necessary, you must consult a professional (including but not limited to your doctor, attorney, financial advisor or such other professional advisor) before using any of the suggested remedies, techniques, or information in this book.

Upon using the contents and information contained in this book, you agree to hold harmless the Author from and against any damages, costs, and expenses, including any legal fees potentially resulting from the application of any of the information provided by this book. This disclaimer applies to any loss, damages or injury caused by the use and application, whether directly or indirectly, of any advice or information presented, whether for breach of contract, tort, negligence, personal injury, criminal intent, or under any other cause of action.

You agree to accept all risks of using the information presented inside this book.

You agree that by continuing to read this book, where appropriate and/or necessary, you shall consult a professional (including but not limited to your doctor, attorney, or financial advisor or such other advisor as needed) before using any of the suggested remedies, techniques, or information in this book.

Table of Contents

INTRODUCTION 10

Chapter 1: What is the Dash Diet 14
    DASH Diet - Real-Life Solutions 14
    The Best Diabetes Diet 15
    What You Need To Know 19

Chapter 2: Principles of Dash Diet 23

Chapter 3: Benefits of the Dash Diet 31

Chapter 4: The importance of exercise during diet 36

Chapter 5: Balancing Nutritional values and macronutrients 49

Chapter 6: Choose a correct diet plan 53

Chapter 7: What to Eat and What to Avoid 58

Chapter 8: Basic Shopping List 63

Chapter 9: A Complete 4 Weeks Diet Meal Plan, day by day 72
    Week 1 72
        Day 1 72
        Day 2 72
        Day 3 72
        Day 4 73
        Day 5 73
        Day 6 73
        Day 7 73
    Week 2 74

- Day 1 74
- Day 2 74
- Day 3 74
- Day 4 74
- Day 5 74
- Day 6 75
- Day 7 75

Week 3 75
- Day 1 75
- Day 2 75
- Day 3 76
- Day 4 76
- Day 5 76
- Day 6 76
- Day 7 76

Week 4 77
- Day 1 77
- Day 2 77
- Day 3 77
- Day 4 77
- Day 5 78
- Day 6 78
- Day 7 78

Chapter 10: Breakfast Dash Recipes 79
- **Whole-grain flax waffles with strawberry purée** 79
- **Spicy baked eggs with goat cheese and spinach** 81
- **Overnight apple and chia seed refrigerator oatmeal** 82
- **Mushroom and asparagus quinoa frittata** 83
- **Ricotta toast with tomato and cucumber** 84
- **Superfood green smoothie** 85
- **Pineapple-banana high-protein smoothie** 86
- **Buckwheat Crepes** 87

Pumpkin Granola Yogurt Parfait..88
Sweet Potato Oat Waffles..90
French Toast...91
Open Face Breakfast Sandwich..92
Egg and Turkey Bacon Breakfast Tacos....................................94
Southwest Tofu Scramble..95
Spinach Mushroom Omelet 96
Almond Banana Breakfast Smoothie 98
Asparagus Omelet Tortilla Wrap...99
Raspberry Peach Puff Pancakes..100
Whole Grain Banana Pancakes..101

Chapter 11: Lunch Dash Recipes....................................105
Vegetable Pasta Soup...105
Tuna Salad..106
Avocado, Strawberry and Melon Salad 107
Mozzarella Stuffed Portobello Mushroom.............................108
Noodles with Spinach, Tofu and Mushroom.........................109
Shrimp Spring Rolls..112
Chicken Wrap..113
Savory Millet Cakes 115
Tuna Melt..117
Goat Cheese and Red Pepper Frittata....................................119
Vegetable Quesadillas with Yoghurt Dips.............................120

Chapter 12: Dinner Dash Recipes 124
Chicken Vegetable Bake..124
Turkey Fajita Bowls...126
Spinach and Quinoa Patties 127
Spicy Seafood Stew..129
Turkey and Vegetables Stir Fry...131
Shepherd's Pie..132

Sweet Pepper Fish and Salsa 133
Pork Tenderloin with Sweet Potatoes and Apples ... 135
Stuffed Peppers.. 137
Thai Steak Salad 139
Thai Chicken Pasta Skillet Recipe 141
Lentil Medley 142
Spiced Salmon 144
Tomato Green Bean Soup 145
Citrus Herb Pot Roast 146
Grilled Tilapia and Pineapple Salsa 148
Mango Rice Pudding... 149
Thai-Style Cobb Salad 151
Vegetable and Turkey Barley Soup............................... 152
Grilled Steak Salad.. 153
Garden Vegetable Beef Soup... 155
Asparagus Soup 157
Sweet Potato and Black Bean Rice Bowl...................... 159
Pesto Corn and Shrimp Salad.. 160
Salmon with Pistachio Horseradish Crust 161
Shredded Pork Salad... 163
White Wine Garlic Chicken 165

Chapter 13: Side Dish Dash Recipes 168
Overnight Oatmeal.. 168
Chili Lime Grilled Pineapple 169
Italian Sausage Stuffed Zucchini.................................... 171
Spicy Almonds 172
Cannellini Bean Hummus 174
Portobello Mushrooms Florentine................................ 175
Asparagus and Horseradish Dip.................................... 176
Peppered Tuna Kebabs 177
Grapefruit, Mint, and Lime Yogurt Parfait 179

Layered Hummus Dip..180
Fruit and Almond Bites 181
Quinoa Veggie Dip..182
Almond Chai Granola 184
Chickpea Mint Tabbouleh...185

Chapter 14: Other Dash Recipes 189
Portobello mushrooms with ricotta, tomato, and mozzarella..189
Pinto bean–stuffed sweet potatoes..190
Roasted vegetables 191
Green beans with toasted almonds..192
Balsamic berries and ricotta...194
Oatmeal dark chocolate chip peanut butter cookies 195

CONCLUSION 198

INTRODUCTION

The DASH diet or the Dietary Approach to Stop Hypertension is a diet that was developed to help reduce high blood pressure. It is for this reason that the foods that can be consumed in this diet are low in sodium. Any individual on a DASH diet will

be able to reduce the risk of developing high blood pressure. The added benefit of the DASH diet is weight loss.

Many health journals and research papers have concluded that specific groups of people must ensure that they limit the sodium in their diet to 1500 milligrams.

- People over the age of 50

- People suffering from kidney diseases or diabetes

- People with high blood pressure

There are certain things to consider when you make a change in your diet. You may be excited about losing weight, but you must ensure that you do not change everything about your lifestyle. Most people are wary of the term diet because they fear that they cannot eat their favorite food. They forget that the diet is not merely a way to lose weight but is a way of life. If you want to start the DASH diet to lose weight, here are a few tips to keep in mind.

- Consult a physician before you begin this diet to understand the changes your body will go through.

- Check your blood pressure at the start of the diet. If you suffer from low blood pressure, consult your physician to understand how this diet can be tweaked to suit your medical condition.

- Check your blood pressure every week when you start the diet.

- Do not throw away all the food at home. Take it slow and get rid of all the junk in your house, one food group at a time.

- If you use butter and oil to cook, swap to olive oil while cooking your meals and use small amounts of oil.

- Always add fruit and vegetables that you like into the diet to make eating fun.

Try to introduce foods that are rich in Vitamin B to keep your body healthy.

- Try to include a bowl of cereal every other day to your diet.

- You should try to reduce the amount of food that you eat every meal. Spread your meals out to ensure that you do not get too bored with the different foods that you eat. When you are on a DASH diet, you will not feel hungry often since the food you consume will satiate your hunger.

- Try to reduce the amount of protein that you consume since too much of anything is not good for you.

- If you need to eat something for a snack, you can always swap the bag of chips with a bowl of fruit or nuts. If you have the time, you can prepare snacks for yourself that are low in fat and sugar.

- The most important thing to remember is to give you a break from the diet at least once a week. This does not mean that you indulge in food that will cancel out all the progress you have made over the week. This is to give you a chance

to take a break from the monotony of the diet and give yourself a treat at the end of the week.

Through the course of the book, you will learn how to cope with the DASH diet and what you should do to lose 30 pounds in 30 days. The book also contains recipes for different meals that adhere to the rules of the DASH diet. We hope you enjoy the recipes and wish you luck on your journey.

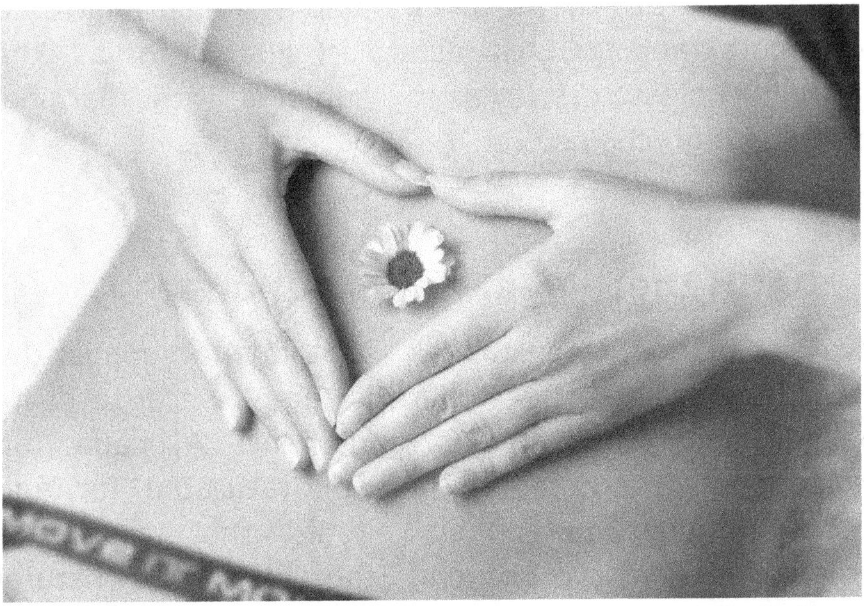

Chapter 1: What is the Dash Diet

Most as of late, researchers took a gander at the DASH diets impact on cholesterol esteems too. It turns out, those hoping to control blood weight and lower cholesterol levels have considerably more motivation to attempt the DASH; the DASH diet essentially lowered aggregate and LDL-cholesterol (alluded to as the "awful" cholesterol) levels in subjects with marginal high and high cholesterol.

DASH Diet - Real-Life Solutions

Avocado plunge, for instance, is a standout amongst the most famous Dash diets there is today, because of its helpful and reasonable arrangement. Avocado, an exceptionally rich source of monosaturated fat and lutein, (cancer prevention agents that assistance protects vision), is among the numerous natural products that are highly-suggested for Dash diet. In this recipe, avocado must be squashed and hollowed, blended with fat-free acrid cream, onion, and hot sauce. This plunge shall be eaten with tortilla chips or cut vegetables. From this dish, a person can get a total of 65 calories, 2 grams protein, 5 grams total fat, 4 grams sugar, 172 milligrams potassium and 31 milligrams calcium. From this, we can infer that a person is sustained a considerable amount of necessary supplements, fundamental for maintaining a well-adjusted diet that is useful for the heart.

In just 14 days, a Dash diet follower will encounter ordinary circulatory strain, with fewer inclinations to eat in-between meals, the real guilty party of weight gain. The Dash diet program additionally teaches individuals to determine the right amount of food intake, the necessary exercise to perform according to age and movement level. Dash instructs and motivates - one of the important reasons why people find it simple to stick to the diet. Additionally, the diet does not require us to quit any pretense of anything significant in our usual diet, instead, it causes us to make a procedure of adjusting to little changes so we can effectively support ourselves.

The Best Diabetes Diet

After some time, many diabetes diet - that is, diets created with the end goal of helping people with diabetes better deal with their diabetes, have been created, had their prime and unobtrusively passed away into bright retirement. Many however remain solid and just as popular as when they were first presented. However, how effective however are these diets.

With the list seeming to develop longer constantly, it frequently leaves a bewildered open pondering where to start. So I chose to do review of the most popular diets currently on the market and toward the finish of that review two diets came through as exceptional entertainers for helping people deal with their diabetes. One of them being the DASH diet. What follows is a brief of what I found out about that diet. However, before we go into that, one might need to ask, what precisely makes up a decent Diabetic diet? The following in this way are just a portion of those components.

1. **It will be low on carbohydrates or if nothing else accommodate a method for either offsetting the sugar through the course of the day or "consuming" off the overabundance, as, through exercise.**
2. **It ought to be high in dietary fiber which has been demonstrated to have numerous health benefits like having a low glycemic record and lowering the probabilities for sicknesses like coronary illness and so on.**
3. **Low in salt. Salt can prompt hypertension-that is high blood pressure, so chopping it down is a must**
4. **Low in fat. Since fat or foods effectively converted to fat like sugars can prompt the individual getting to be overweight-a risk factor for diabetes, usually essential for such sustenance to have a low-fat substance.**

5. A decent diabetic diet ought to endeavor to meet the recommended daily allowance for potassium. Potassium is important because it can turn around the negative effects on the circulatory framework that salt has.

Anyway that isn't the extent that its advantages go. The diet has additionally been observed to be similarly efficacious as a diabetes diet. In fact, in a review of 35 diets did by US News and World report recently it turned out joint first with The Biggest Loser diet as the best diabetes diet. Mirroring much of the advice offered by the American Diabetes Association, it has been shown to show both diabetes avoidance and control characteristics.

On counteractive action, it has been shown to enable individuals to get in shape and furthermore keep it off. Since being overweight is a major risk factor for creating Type 2 diabetes, this quality shows it off as an extraordinary diabetes diet alternative.

What's more, the risk factors related with metabolic disorder, a condition which builds the odds of creating diabetes is likewise diminished by a blend of the DASH diet and calorie restriction. As regards control, the results of a small study published in a 2011 edition of Diabetes Care uncovered that Type 2 diabetics following two months on DASH had decreased their dimensions of A1C and their fasting blood sugar.

Also the diet has been observed to be more adaptable than most, a fact that would make it simpler to follow and adjustable, to empower it agree to a specialist's dietary advice to his diabetic patient.

Another favorable position offered by this diet is the dimension of its adjustment to dietary rules. Light as it might appear, this is actually important because a few diets place a restriction on specific foods, along these lines leaving the individual possibly insufficient in specific nutrients and minerals.

A breakdown of this congruity demonstrates that where fat is concerned, the diet satisfactorily falls inside the 20 to 35 percent of daily calories recommended by the administration. It likewise meets the 10 percent maximum limit dispensed to immersed fat by falling admirably below that. It likewise meets the recommended amount of proteins and carbohydrates.

Where salt is concerned, it has rule feast tops for this mineral. Both for the recommended daily maximum of 2,300 mg and in case you're African-American, are 51 years or more seasoned or have hypertension, diabetes or unending kidney illness, the 1,500 mg limit.

Different nutrients are enough dealt with additionally by this diet. Thus the recommended daily intake of 22 to 34 grams' fiber for adults is very much accommodated by this diet. So too is potassium, a nutrient that is set apart for its ability to counter salts blood pressure raising characteristics, diminish the risk of creating kidney stones and furthermore decline bone misfortune. Impressively so because of the difficulty in normally procuring the recommended daily intake-4,700 mg or the equivalent of eating 11 bananas every day.

Recommended daily intake of Vitamin D for adults who don't get enough sunlight is penciled down at 15 mg. However, the diet falls just short of this, it is recommended that this can be effectively made up by state a nutrient D invigorated grain.

Calcium so vital for solid bones and teeth, blood vessel generation and muscle work is additionally enough dealt with by the diet. The administration's recommendation of between 1,000 mg to 1300 mg is met here effectively with no affectation or graces. The equivalent goes for Vitamin B-12. The administration's recommendation is 2.4 mg. The diets arrangement is 6.7.

What You Need To Know

There is a specific eating plan that has been proven to bring down hypertension or high pulse. This diet is known as the DASH or Dietary Approaches to Stop Hypertension.

What is DASH diet?

The DASH diet is a consequence of clinical examinations directed by researchers of the National Heart, Lung and Blood Institute (NHLBI). The researchers discovered that a diet high in potassium, magnesium, calcium, protein and fiber, and low in fat and cholesterol can radically decrease high circulatory strain.

The investigation demonstrated that a diet rich in vegetables, fruits and low-fat dairy items had a major impact in diminishing hypertension. It additionally demonstrated that the DASH diet produces fast outcomes, sometimes in as meager as about fourteen days in the wake of beginning the diet.

The DASH diet additionally underlines on three significant supplements: magnesium, calcium and potassium. These minerals are thought to help lessen high circulatory strain. A normal 2,000-calorie diet contains 500 milligrams of magnesium, 4.7 grams of potassium and 1.2 grams of calcium.

Doing the DASH Diet

Following the DASH diet is exceptionally simple and takes little time in the choice and planning of dinners. Foods rich in fats and cholesterol are maintained a strategic distance from.

Since the foods you eat in a DASH diet are high in fiber content, it is suggested that you gradually increment your utilization of fiber-rich sustenance to evade loose bowels and other stomach related issues. You can bit by bit increment your fiber intake by eating an additional serving of fruits and vegetables in each dinner.

If you choose to eat meat, limit your utilization to just six ounces per day, which is comparable in size to a deck of cards. You can likewise eat more vegetables, cereals, pasta and beans into your meat dishes. Low-fat milk or skim milk is likewise a great source of protein without the excess fat and cholesterol.

For snacks, you can attempt canned or dried fruits, just as crisp ones. There are additionally healthy snack alternatives for those on the DASH diet, for example, graham saltines, unsalted nuts and low-fat yogurt.

It's Easy to DASH

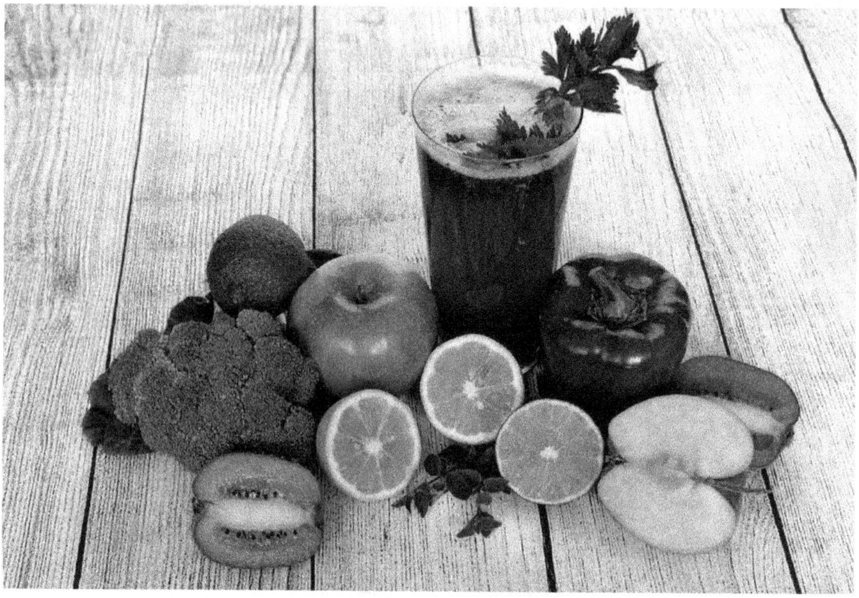

Chapter 2: Principles of Dash Diet

Whole Grains and Starchy Vegetables

Whole grains and starchy vegetables are good sources of fiber, helping to slow the absorption of glucose in the blood. Packed with vitamins and minerals, these foods should always be chosen over refined and processed carbohydrates. Whole grains include brown rice, barley, farro, quinoa, oats, and whole-grain pasta; starchy vegetables include potatoes and sweet potatoes.

Servings: Aim for four to six servings daily. One serving equates to one-half cup of cooked grains, one slice of whole grain bread, or one medium-size sweet potato.

Helpful Tips and Tricks: Short on time or don't want to cook? No problem! Instead of making a pot of brown rice, you can look for precooked, frozen whole grains in your grocer's freezer aisle.

Fruits and Vegetables

Fruits and vegetables are a vital part of the Mediterranean DASH diet. Full of vitamins, minerals, and antioxidants, these are nutrient powerhouses in our day-to-day life. These fiber-rich foods help us feel full and satisfied, support lower blood pressure and weight management, and help ward off a variety of diseases. Be sure to eat plenty of alliums, such as garlic, onions, and leeks, as well as a good amount of crucifers, including broccoli, cauliflower, and Brussels sprouts, on a weekly basis.

Servings: Aim to consume at least four to five servings of vegetables and three servings of fruit daily. One serving equates to one-half cup of fruit or cooked vegetables, or one cup of raw leafy greens.

Helpful Tips and Tricks: Fresh and frozen will be your go-to foundation, but canned and packed in water or natural juices are great to keep on hand as a backup option. And don't forget dried fruit, a great addition to your yogurt or oatmeal or sprinkled on top of a salad!

Building a Plate

Traditional Mediterranean cuisine is enjoyed as part of a balanced lifestyle, which includes a sustainable approach to eating well. The cornerstone of any healthy diet is a properly proportioned plate. Fruits and vegetables are eaten in plenty, while meats, sweet treats, and wine are enjoyed in moderation. A balanced plate should be one-half non-starchy vegetables, one-quarter whole grains or starchy vegetables, and one-quarter lean protein.

Lean Proteins: Animal and Plant

Lean proteins encompass both animal and plant-based protein sources. In the Mediterranean DASH diet, we place a heavier emphasis on fish and shellfish, with smaller portions of eggs, lean poultry, and meat. When selecting beef, pork, and other animal protein, look for leaner cuts, such as loin and round. These cuts of meat are flavorful and easy to prepare while also being lower in saturated fat. Eggs and poultry are largely excellent choices as well.

Plant-based protein sources are superstars. They are high in fiber and complex carbohydrates while being low in fat. They are also sources of other key minerals and nutrients, such as potassium, magnesium, folate, and iron. Plant-based proteins include beans and legumes, such as lentils, peas, and soy. For our purposes, nuts and seeds will also be part of this category, contributing lean protein and healthy fats.

Servings: Aim to get up to six ounces per day of lean meat, poultry, or seafood. Think of a three-ounce portion as the size of a deck of playing cards. Try to get two to three servings of seafood on a weekly basis. Aim for four to five servings of nuts, seeds, beans, and legumes per week. One serving is about one-half cup cooked beans or legumes, three ounces of tempeh or tofu, and one-third cup of nuts and seeds.

Helpful Tips and Tricks: Keep low-sodium versions of canned tuna, salmon, and beans on hand to help get meals on the table quickly and easily.

Healthy Fats and Oils

Olives and olive oil are staples in the Mediterranean DASH diet, known for their heart-healthy monounsaturated fat content and anti-inflammatory properties. For a more neutral-flavored oil, canola oil is a good choice.

Another great source of healthy fat is the avocado. Research has shown that the high levels of oleic acid found in avocados help decrease LDL, the "bad" cholesterol, and boost HDL, the "good" cholesterol.

Servings: Aim for two to three servings of fats and oils daily. One serving equates to one teaspoon of oil or one-quarter of an avocado.

Helpful Tips and Tricks: Making your own salad dressing is a great way to incorporate flavorful, low-sodium versions into your daily routine. Use empty jam or nut butter jars to make larger batches, which will keep in the refrigerator for a couple of weeks.

Low-Fat Dairy

Low-fat dairy foods such as cheese and yogurt are foundational foods in the Mediterranean DASH diet. The dairy group contributes important nutrients, including calcium, vitamin D, and potassium. Studies have shown that fermented dairy products, such as yogurt and some cheeses, have an inverse relationship with cardiovascular disease and type 2 diabetes. There is some evidence that eating fermented dairy foods may help fight inflammation associated with the development of heart disease.

Servings: Aim to consume two to three servings of low-fat dairy daily. One serving equates to one cup of nonfat or low-fat plain yogurt (includes Greek yogurt) or one-and-a-half ounces of cheese.

Helpful Tips and Tricks: Have a hankering for tuna salad? Use plain yogurt in place of mayonnaise to add protein, flavor, and richness without the added saturated fat and calories. Yogurt can also be added to foods like soup and oatmeal to increase the protein content and add creaminess without using butter or heavy cream.

Limited Added Sugar

The Mediterranean DASH diet naturally decreases sugar intake without making you feel deprived in any way. Dessert and sweet treats can still be part of your weekly routine, but with a focus on natural sources of sugar, such as fruit sugars, honey, and maple syrup.

Servings: Aim to limit sugar to five or fewer servings per week. One serving size equals one tablespoon of maple syrup or honey, or one-half cup of ice cream or frozen yogurt.

Helpful Tips and Tricks: Try adding fresh or dried fruit and a teaspoon of jam to a bowl of oatmeal or yogurt in place of sugar.

Limited Sodium

Many foods naturally contain some sodium. However, much of the sodium many of us consume is added to foods, making it too easy for most people to overconsume. You can find it hiding in most processed foods and often added in huge quantities to restaurant meals. Excessive sodium intake is one of the main drivers of high blood pressure. Using less salt, and instead relying on herbs and spices to add bold flavor to foods, is a key component of the Mediterranean DASH diet.

Servings: Aim to consume between 1,500 and 2,300 milligrams of sodium per day. For reference, one-quarter teaspoon of kosher salt equals about 500 milligrams of sodium.

Helpful Tips and Tricks: Reach for herbs and spices to create depth of flavor, adding salt in small amounts. You can always add salt, but once it's there you cannot take it away!

The recipes included in the Mediterranean DASH diet follow these guidelines:

Snacks, sides, and desserts: ≤300 milligrams of sodium

Entrées and meals: ≤570 milligrams of sodium

SNEAKY SODIUM

To keep your sodium intake in check, it is essential to be able to properly read a food label. The first step is to become familiar with portion sizing (i.e., if you eat two servings worth of a food, you double your sodium intake). As with sugar, it is important to recognize the difference between naturally occurring sodium in foods and added salt. Some foods, like celery, beets, and milk, organically contain sodium in low levels, which supply our bodies with electrolytes. Added salt is salt added during cooking and processing, and this is what accounts for most of our daily sodium intake. Examples of foods typically loaded with added salt include canned foods, cured and deli-style meats, cheeses, frozen prepared meals, soups, chips, and condiments. To help prevent excessive sodium intake, look for foods labeled "no salt added," "low-sodium," or "sodium-free." When using canned items, such as beans and lentils, rinse well with water prior to using. And try using garlic, citrus juice, herbs, and spices for flavor before reaching for the saltshaker.

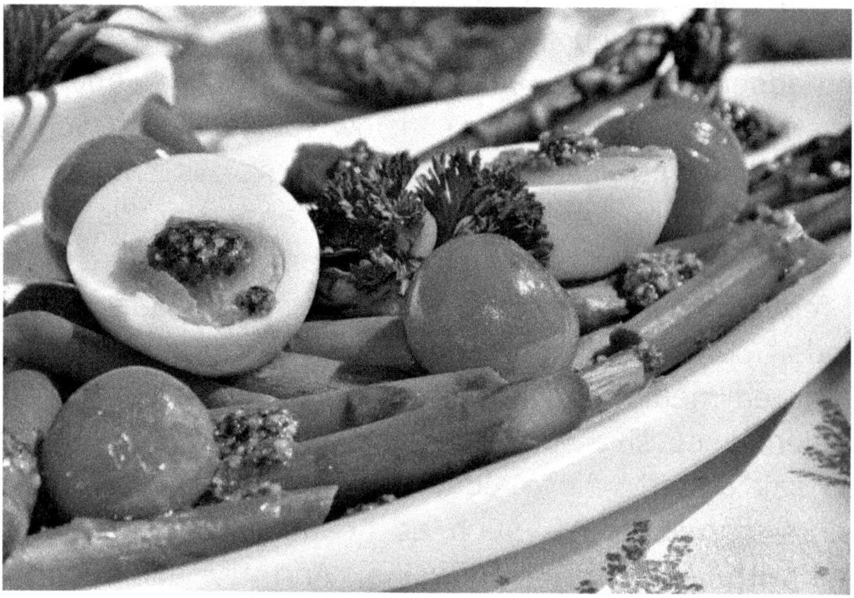

Chapter 3: Benefits of the Dash Diet

The DASH diet comes with a range of health benefits. Following are some of the major advantages of following the DASH diet:

Cardiovascular Health

The DASH diet decreases your consumption of refined carbohydrates by increasing your consumption of foods high in potassium and dietary fiber (fruits, vegetables, and whole grains). In addition, it diminishes your consumption of saturated fats. Therefore, the DASH diet has a favorable effect on your lipid profile and glucose tolerance, which reduces the prevalence of metabolic syndrome (MS) in post-menopausal women.

Reports state that a diet limited to 500 calories favors a loss of 17% of total body weight in 6 months in overweight women. This reduces the prevalence of MS by 15%. However, when this diet follows the patterns of the DASH diet, while triglycerides decrease in a similar way, the reduction in weight and BP is even greater.

It also reduces blood sugar and increases HDL, which decreases the prevalence of MS in 35% of women. These results contrast with those of other studies, which have reported that the DASH diet alone, i.e., without caloric restriction, does not affect HDL and glycemia. This means that the effects of the DASH diet on MS are associated mainly with the greater reduction in BP and that, for more changes, the diet would be required to be combined with weight loss.

Helpful for Patients with Diabetes

The DASH diet has also been shown to help reduce inflammatory and coagulation factors (C-reactive protein and fibrinogen) in patients with diabetes. These benefits are associated with the contribution of antioxidants and fibers, given the high consumption of fruits and vegetables that the DASH diet requires. In addition, the DASH diet has been shown to reduce total cholesterol and LDL, which reduces the estimated 10-year cardiovascular risk. Epidemiological studies have determined that women in the highest quintile of food consumption according to the DASH diet have a 24% to 33% lower risk of coronary events and an 18% lower risk of a cerebrovascular event. Similarly, a meta-analysis of six observational studies has determined that the DASH diet can reduce the risk of cardiovascular events by 20%.

Weight Reduction

Limited research associates the DASH diet, in isolation, with weight reduction. In some studies, weight reduction was greater when the subject was on the DASH diet as compared to an isocaloric controlled diet. This could be related to the higher calcium intake and lower energy density of the DASH diet. The American guidelines for the treatment of obesity emphasize that, regardless of diet, a caloric restriction would be the most important factor in reducing weight.

However, several studies have made an association between (1) greater weight and fat loss in diets and (2) caloric restriction and higher calcium intake. Studies have also observed an inverse association between dairy consumption and body mass index (BMI). In obese patients, weight loss has been reported as being 170% higher after 24 weeks on a hypocaloric diet with high calcium intake.

In addition, the loss of trunk fat was reported to be 34% of the total weight loss as compared to only 21% in a control diet. It has also been determined that a calcium intake of 20 mg per gram has a protective effect in overweight middle-aged women. This would be equivalent to 1275 mg of calcium for a western diet of 1700 kcal. It has been suggested that low calcium intake increases the circulating level of the parathyroid hormone and vitamin D, which have been shown to increase the level of cytosolic calcium in adipocytes in vitro, changing the metabolism of lipolysis to lipogenesis.

Despite these reports, the effect that diet-provided calcium has on women's weight after menopause is a controversial subject. An epidemiological study has noted that a sedentary lifestyle and, to a lesser extent, caloric intake are associated with post- menopausal weight gain, though calcium intake is not associated with it. The average calcium intake in this group of women is approximately 1000 mg, which would be low, as previously stated. Another study of post-menopausal women shows that calcium and vitamin D supplementation in those with a calcium intake of less than 1200 mg per day decreases the risk of weight gain by 11%.

In short, the DASH diet is favorable, both in weight control and in the regulation of fatty tissue deposits, due to its high calcium content (1200 mg/day). The contribution of calcium apparently plays a vital role in the regulation of lipogenesis.

Now that we have established the myriad benefits of the DASH diet, let's check out some of the most delicious and unique DASH diet recipes for all times of the day!

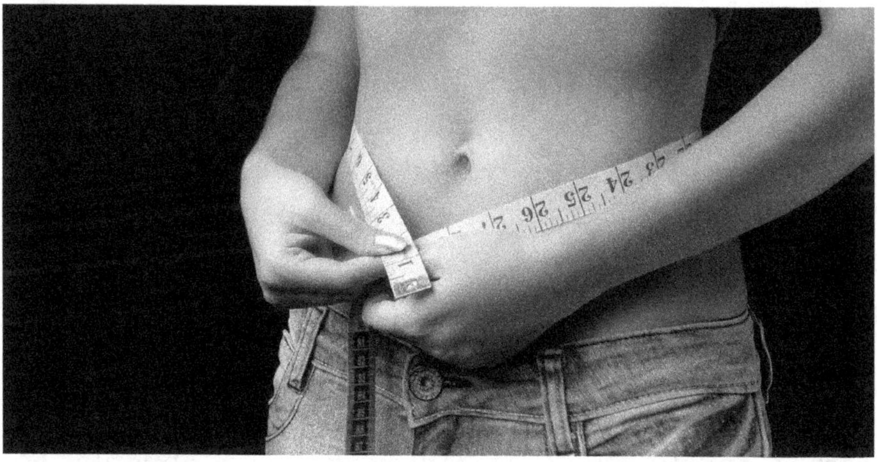

Chapter 4: The importance of exercise during diet

Exercise is good for human health in many ways, regardless of what you choose to do. My goal in this section is not only to gently introduce you to the numerous health benefits that regular physical activity can offer but also to remind you that your 28-day plan will include a diverse, varied exercise routine that I hope provides options that everyone can get something out of.

Although the DASH diet focuses on food choices, there is no denying that regular and varied exercise represents an important component of a healthy lifestyle and one that can confer additional benefits. For those of you who are starting from square one, you should know that any exercise is better than none and that there is absolutely nothing wrong with starting slowly and easing into a more rigorous routine. With that being said, the CDC identifies moderate intensity aerobic activity that totals 120 to 150 minutes weekly, in combination with two additional weekly days of muscular resistance training, as an ideal combination to confer numerous health benefits to adults. Per the CDC, these benefits include the following:

Better weight management: When combined with dietary modification, regular physical activity plays a role in supporting or enhancing weight-management efforts. Regular exercise is a great way to expend calories on top of any dietary changes you will be making on this program.

Reduced risk for cardiovascular disease: A reduction in blood pressure is a well-recognized benefit of regular physical activity, which ultimately contributes to a reduced risk of cardiovascular disease.

Reduced risk of type 2 diabetes: Regular physical activity is known to improve blood glucose control and insulin sensitivity.

Improved mood: Regular physical activity is associated with improvements in mood and reductions in anxiety owing to the manner in which exercise positively influences the biochemistry of the human brain by releasing hormones and affecting neurotransmitters.

Better sleep: Those who exercise more regularly tend to sleep better than those who don't, which may be partially owing to the reductions in stress and anxiety that often occur in those who exercise regularly.

Stronger bones and muscles: Combining cardiovascular and resistance training confers serious benefits to both your bones and your muscles, which keep your body functioning at a high level as you age.

A longer life span: Those who exercise regularly tend to enjoy a lower risk of chronic disease and a longer life span.

As you will see in the 28-day plan, your recommended exercise totals will be met by exercising four out of the seven days a week. The exercise days will be broken up as follows: All four of the active days will include aerobic exercise for 30 minutes. As a beginner, I encourage you to start slowly and build up to the four days. Two of the four active days will also include strength training. The bottom line is that you don't have to exercise for hours each day to enjoy the health benefits of physical activity. Our goal with this plan is to make the health benefits of exercise as accessible and attainable as possible for those who are ready and willing to give it a try. Before we get to the good stuff, though, there is still a lot of wisdom to be shared about getting the most out of your workouts.

GETTING THE MOST OUT OF YOUR WORKOUTS

Just as with healthy eating strategies, there are certainly important things to keep in mind about physical activity that will help support your long-term success. Let's take a look at a few important considerations that will help you get the most out of your workouts:

Rest days: Even though we haven't even started, I'm going to preach the importance of good rest. Don't forget that you are taking part in this journey to improve your health for the long term, not to burn yourself out in 28 days. Although some of you with more experience with exercise may feel confident going above and beyond, my best advice for the majority of those reading is to listen to your body and take days off to minimize risk of injury and burnout.

Stretching: Stretching is a great way to prevent injury and keep you pain-free both during workouts and in daily life. Whether it's a deliberate activity after a workout or through additional means such as yoga, stretching is beneficial in many ways.

Enjoyment: There is no right or wrong style of exercise. You are being provided a diverse plan that emphasizes a variety of different cardiovascular and resistance training exercises. If there are certain activities within these groups that you don't enjoy, it's okay not to do them. Your ability to stick with regular physical activity in the long term will depend on finding a style of exercise that you enjoy.

Your limits: Physical activity is good for you, and it should be fun, too. It's up to you to keep it that way. While it is important to challenge yourself, don't risk injury by taking things too far too fast.

Your progress: Although this is not an absolute requirement, some of you reading may find joy and fulfillment through tracking your exercise progress and striving toward a longer duration, more repetitions, and so on. If you are the type who enjoys a competitive edge, it may be fun to find a buddy to exercise and progress with.

Warm-ups: Last but certainly not least, your exercise routine will benefit greatly from a proper warm-up routine, which includes starting slowly or doing exercises similar to the ones included in your workout, but at a lower intensity.

SET A ROUTINE

The exercise part of the DASH plan was developed with CDC exercise recommendations in mind in order to support your best health. For some, the 28-day plan may seem like a lot; for others it may not seem like that much. If we look at any exercise routine from a very general perspective, there are at least three broad categories to be aware of.

Strength training: This involves utilizing your muscles against some form of counterweight, which may be your own body or dumbbells. These types of activities alter your resting metabolic rate by supporting the development of muscle while also strengthening your bones.

Aerobic exercise: Also known as cardiovascular activity, these are the quintessential exercises such as jogging or running that involve getting your body moving and getting your heart rate up.

Mobility, flexibility, and balance: Stretching after workouts or even devoting your exercise time on one day a week to stretching or yoga is a great way to maintain mobility and prevent injury in the long term.

This routine recommends involving a combination of both cardiovascular and resistance training. You will be provided with a wide array of options to choose from to accommodate a diverse exercise routine. My best recommendation is to settle on the types of exercises that offer a balance between enjoyment and challenge. Remember that the benefits of physical activity are to be enjoyed well beyond just your 28-day plan, and the best way to ensure that is the case is selecting movements you truly enjoy. My final recommendation in this regard is to also include some form of stretching either after your workouts or on a rest day.

Cardio and Body Weight Exercises

Your 28-day plan will be built around the cardiovascular and strength-training exercises that are detailed in this section. In addition to a variety of different cardiovascular exercise options, the strength-training options you will be provided are divided into four distinct categories: core, lower body, upper body, and full body. Per your sample routine, an ideal strength workout will include one exercise from each of these categories:

CARDIO

Brisk walking: This is essentially walking at a pace beyond your normal walking rate for a purpose beyond just getting from point A to point B.

Jogging: This is the intermediary stage between brisk walking and running and can be used as an accompaniment to either exercise, depending on your fitness level.

Running: The quintessential and perhaps most well-recognized cardiovascular exercise.

Jumping jacks: Although 30 minutes straight of jumping jacks may be impractical, they are a good complement to the other activities on this list.

Dancing: Those who have a background in dancing may enjoy using it to their advantage, but anyone can put on their favorite songs and dance like there's nobody watching.

Jump rope: Own a jump rope? Why not use it as part of your cardiovascular workout? It is a fun way to get your cardio in.

Other options (equipment permitting): Activities like rowing, swimming and water aerobics, biking, and using elliptical and stair climbing machines can be great ways to exercise.

In order to meet the CDC guidelines, your goal will be to work up to a total of 30 minutes of cardiovascular activity per workout session. You may use a combination of the exercises listed. I suggest that beginners should start with brisk walking or jogging—whatever activity you are most comfortable with.

CORE

Plank: The plank is a classic core exercise that focuses on stability and strength of the muscles in the abdominal and surrounding areas. Engage your buttocks, press your forearms into the ground, and hold for 60 seconds. Beginners may start with a 15- to 30-second hold and work their way up.

Side plank: Another core classic and a plank variation that focuses more on the oblique muscles on either side of your central abdominals. Keep the buttocks tight, and prevent your torso from sagging to get the most out of this exercise.

Wood chopper: A slightly more dynamic movement that works the rotational functionality of your core and mimics chopping a log of wood. You can start with little to no weight until you feel comfortable and progress from there. Start the move with feet shoulder width apart, back straight, and slightly crouched. If you are using weight, hold it with both hands next to the outside of either thigh, twist to the side, and lift the weight across and upward, keeping your arms straight and turning your torso such that you end up with the weight above your opposite shoulder.

LOWER BODY

Goblet squat: Start your stance with feet slightly wider than shoulder width and a dumbbell held tightly with both hands in front of your chest. Sit back into a squat, hinging at both the knee and the hip joint, and lower your legs until they are parallel to the ground. Push up through your heels to the starting position and repeat. Use a chair to squat onto if you don't feel comfortable.

Dumbbell walking lunge: Start upright with a dumbbell in each hand and feet in your usual standing position. Step forward with one leg and sink down until your back knee is just above the ground. Remain upright and ensure the front knee does not bend over the toes. Push through the heel of the front foot and step forward and through with your rear foot. Start with no weights, and add weight as you feel comfortable.

Romanian dead lift: Unlike the squat and lunge, the Romanian dead lift puts the primary emphasis on the rear muscles of the legs (hamstrings). Stand in a similar starting position to walking lunges, but this time you will hinge at the hips and push your buttocks and hip backward while naturally lowering the dumbbells in front of you. Squeeze your buttocks on the ascent back to the starting position. You can also do this exercise on one leg to improve balance and increase core activation—however, you may need to use lighter weights.

UPPER BODY

Push-ups: These are the ultimate body-weight exercise and can be done just about anywhere. You will want to set up with your hands just beyond shoulder width, keeping your body in a straight line and always engaging your core as you ascend and descend, without letting your elbows flare out. Those who struggle to perform push-ups consecutively can start by performing them on their knees or even against a wall if regular push-ups sound like too much.

Dumbbell shoulder press: A great exercise for upper-body and shoulder strength. Bring a pair of dumbbells to ear level, palms forward, and straighten your arms overhead.

FULL BODY

Mountain climbers: On your hands and feet, keep your body in a straight line, with your abdominal and buttocks muscles engaged, similar to the top position of a push-up. Rapidly alternate pulling your knees into your chest while keeping your core tight. Continue in this left, right, left, right rhythm as if you are replicating a running motion. Always try to keep your spine in a straight line.

Push press: This is essentially a combination move incorporating a partial squat and a dumbbell shoulder press. Using a weight that you are comfortable with, stand feet slightly beyond shoulder width, with light dumbbells held in a pressing position. Descend for a squat to a depth you feel comfortable with, and on the ascent simultaneously push the dumbbells overhead.

Burpee (advanced/optional): This is a classic full-body exercise that is essentially a dynamic combination of a push-up, a squat, and a jump. This particular exercise is very effective but may be challenging for some and should be utilized only by those who feel comfortable. The proper sequencing of the movement involves starting from a standing position before lowering into a squat, placing your hands on the floor, and jumping backward to land on the balls of your feet while keeping your core strong. Jump back to your hands and jump again into the air, reaching your hands upward.

Stay Hydrated

Proper hydration by drinking water is an important habit that supports good health and weight management. Caloric drinks with minimal nutrients, like soda, have become an increasingly common source of calories in our population, and replacing such beverages with plain drinking water is a valuable step to take toward better health. Using natural flavors like a splash of lemon is a good way to transition from drinking sweetened beverages to plain water. It is recommended that women drink about 11 cups a day and men drink about 14 cups a day. Keep in mind that this includes fluid from both foods and beverages, not just water. Certain types of food, especially fruit and certain vegetables, have very high water contents. Beverages such as coffee, tea, and carbonated water also count toward your daily totals. Drinking enough water will also help prevent constipation and work together with the fiber from your diet to keep your bowels working effectively.

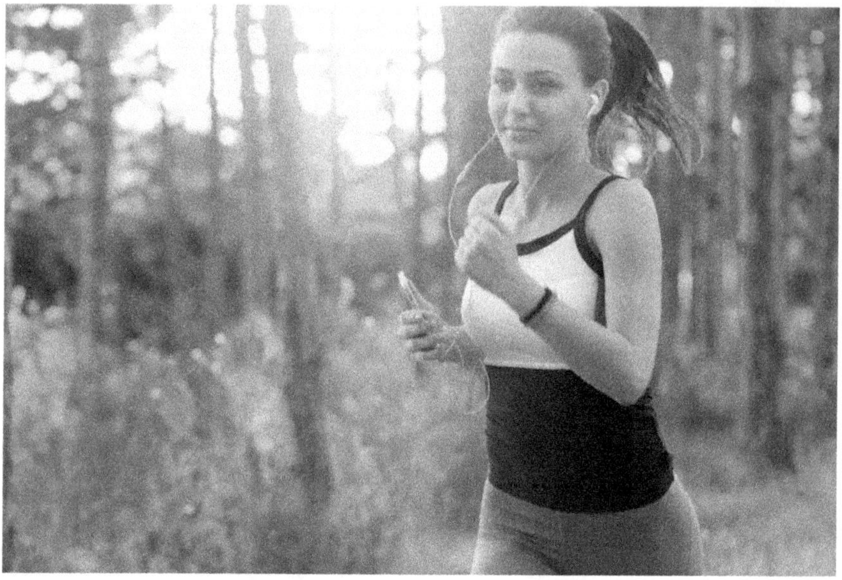

Chapter 5: Balancing Nutritional values and macronutrients

According to the World Health Organization, unhealthy diets and excessive energy intakes are among the primary drivers for chronic disease worldwide. Nutrition is the first and arguably most important pillar of your holistic approach to healthier living. Thus far I have spoken at great length about both the DASH diet and its ability to offer you a path to lower blood pressure as well as about the science of calories and how managing your caloric intake is an important step to take on the path toward weight loss. As you will see in the chapters to come, your 28-day DASH diet plan keeps this in mind while also offering you support for the other major pillars of health, including exercise, sleep, and stress management.

EXERCISE

As Hippocrates said, "Walking is man's best medicine." There is no question about the strong association that exists between exercise and good health. Regular physical activity is good for your heart and a key component to living a longer and healthier life. A 2012 article published in the journal ISRN Cardiology claimed that burning about 1,000 kcal per week through physical activity represents the threshold beyond which exercise can have a tangible positive effect on longevity.

Keep in mind that you can burn this number of calories in a week simply by walking an hour a day at the pace of about three and a half miles per hour. In other words, it's important to realize you don't need to be an all-star athlete to enjoy the benefits of exercise. Further to this point, a large 2017 study published in The Lancet found that both recreational and nonrecreational physical activity are linked with a lower risk of heart disease.

STRESS MANAGEMENT

According to an American Psychological Association (APA) survey from 2010, 44 percent of Americans reported increased stress levels over the past five years. It's impossible to deny that stress is a pervasive component of daily life for many Americans and one that can have profound negative consequences on blood pressure, body weight, and overall health.

Above all else, stress is simply unpleasant to endure in the long term. It may be unavoidable, and it's something we all have to face from time to time, but that does not change the fact that learning how to properly manage stress is an important area of concern and one that will be discussed at greater length as part of the 28-day plan in order to help facilitate your overall success with the DASH diet.

SLEEP

There is no question that sleeping well is a very underrated cornerstone of good health. Even if everything else is going perfectly, if you are consistently sleeping too little it will probably be challenging for you to truly feel your best. Perhaps unsurprisingly, the CDC statistics suggest that one in three Americans does not reach the minimum recommendation of seven hours of sleep.

Why is this a particular problem when it comes to high blood pressure? A 2013 systematic review published in the journal **Current Pharmaceutical Design** found that insufficient sleep is linked with an increased risk of high blood pressure and hypertension. The researchers behind this particular study believe this may be due to excessive stimulation of your body's systems when too many hours are spent in a waking state, which acts as a kind of blood-pressure-raising stress, not necessarily different from other stressors one might face in daily life.

It doesn't end there, though. There is mounting evidence that sleep plays an important role in modulating your metabolism, especially as it relates to how your body responds to key hormones such as insulin, ghrelin, and leptin. According to a 2011 review in **Current Opinion in Clinical Nutrition and Metabolic Care**, a lack of sleep may also be associated with increased hunger and appetite, which may partially explain a potential relationship between sleep loss and weight gain.

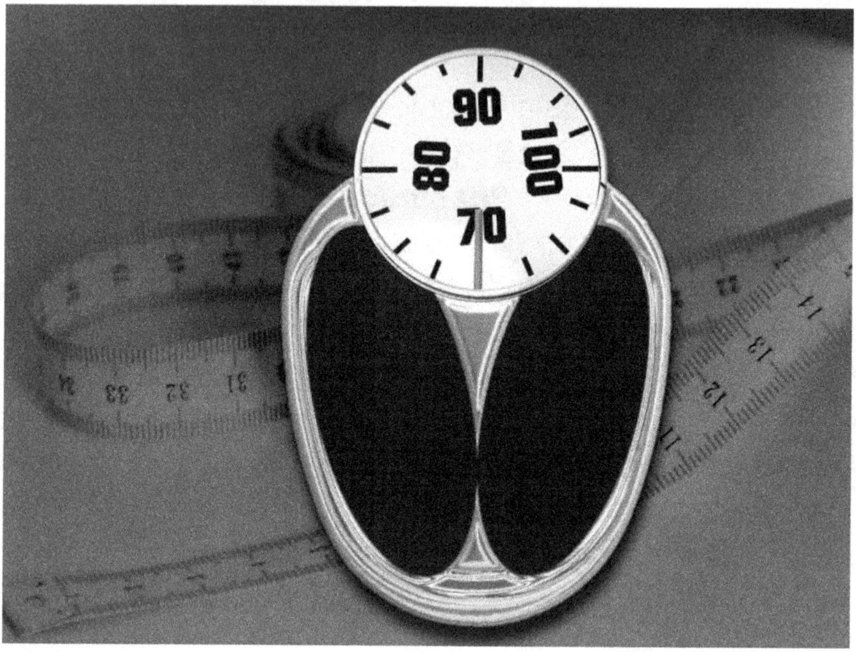
90
80
100
70

Chapter 6: Choose a correct diet plan

The DASH diet plan focus on expanding vegetables, fruits, entire grains, and vegetables; picking lean meats, low-fat dairy, nuts and solid fats; and constraining included sugars, trans fats, included salt, and prepared foods. Serving sizes from every food group depend on individual calorie needs.

Nutrients Per Day:

- Grains: 6 servings
- Vegetables: 3-4 servings
- Fruits: 4 servings
- Low-Fat or Fat-Free Dairy: 2-3 servings
- Lean Meat, Poultry, or Fish: 4 ounces or less
- Fat/oils: 2 servings
- Sodium: 2300 mg or less

Nutrients Per Week:

- Nuts, seeds, and legumes: 3-4 times per week
- Sweets and added sugars: 3 servings or less

The secret to DASH's prosperity is its emphasis on increasing vegetables, fruits, and whole foods that are normally low in sodium and high in potassium. While most realize that reducing sodium is essential, many don't realize that getting adequate potassium intake is similarly as key for managing blood pressure.

At the point when foods are handled, their potassium levels really decline. In this way, picking whole or negligibly prepared foods can improve blood pressure regulation from both a sodium and a potassium viewpoint. In addition, you'll, as a rule, decline your intake of soaked fat, included sugars, and generally calories—all of which can enable you to get thinner and keep it off for good.

So—Why Does DASH Have So Few Followers?

Misconception #1: The DASH Diet is Only for People With High Blood Pressure.

The DASH diet was made when researchers were searching for ways to viably reduce hypertension, however, this was more than 20 years back! Despite the fact that it's still regularly advertised as a treatment for hypertension, the DASH eating plan is extremely a perfect method to eat for by and large wellbeing, weight support, and incessant disease aversion.

Additionally, individuals with hypertension aren't the main ones who need to stress over sodium admission. Data suggests that 90 percent of Americans exceed sodium's maximum breaking point (3500mg) day by day. Routinely going over this amount negatively affects your body—even healthy bodies—after some time.

Misconception #2: "Low-Sodium" and "No-Salt" are the DASH Diet's Sole Focus.

Sodium reduction is part of the DASH equation, yet it's by all account, not the only core interest. Eating by DASH recommendations likewise builds your intake of potassium, calcium, magnesium, and fiber—all nutrients that assume a job in cardiovascular wellbeing, just as the avoidance of other constant maladies. It's believed to be the combination of expanding your intake of these nutrients and diminishing your intake of included sugar, salt, sodium and unfortunate fats that prompts lower circulatory strain and a clothing rundown of other long haul medical advantages.

Likewise, diminishing sodium doesn't limit you to exhausting, flat nourishment, nor does it mean you need to hurl out the salt shaker. Indeed, diminishing the amount of salt you use and picking lower-sodium products are key, yet opting for new nourishments or entire sustenances rather than boxed, canned, and prepared to-warm things has a major enough effect. Experiment with flavors and herbs, and utilize a little salt to upgrade season. Salt ought to never be the sole enhancing or flavoring in any in the dish.

Misconception #3: The DASH Diet is Unapproachable.

This is overwhelming for many (myself included), yet there are plenty of traps and tips to support you. First, comprehend that "entire foods" doesn't solely mean new produce. Exploit time-saving, minimally handled foods like unseasoned frozen vegetables and no-salt-included canned veggies.

Two extra easy routes that can undoubtedly be worked into a DASH diet plan are meal preparing and bunch cooking—the two of which are significant for quick, healthy eating. Meal preparing doesn't need to mean preparing a full meal, either. It's simply getting ready components that can be utilized to hurl together a quick meal—like preparing chicken bosoms, broiling vegetables, and cooking an entire grain like quinoa. You can likewise minimize time spent in the kitchen by purchasing weekly salad greens, bags of pre-cut veggies, and preparing produce toward the beginning of the week.

Misconception #4: DASH is a "Diet" That You Follow Intermittently

Maybe the biggest thing that keeps people away from the following DASH is approaching it with a "win or bust" frame of mind. However, DASH does not fall under the common "diet" approach of following an eating plan for half a month and after that coming back to your old method for eating. All things considered, nobody's diet is immaculate. Like the Mediterranean Diet, the DASH diet is best seen as a solid method for living and eating. Making little, gradual changes in your food decisions—and food quality—can enable you to frame healthier habits forever.

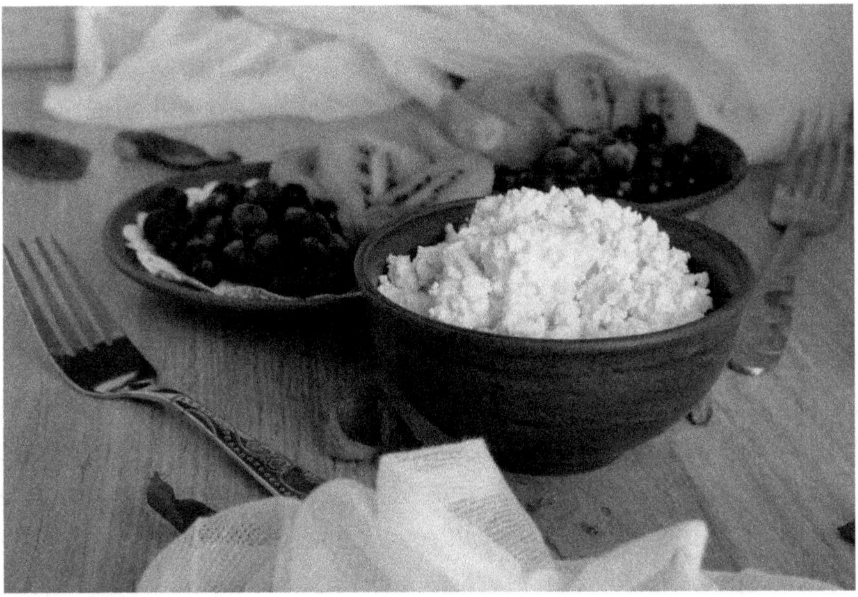

Chapter 7: What to Eat and What to Avoid

Foods Allowed On The DASH Diet

The following foods should be consumed daily to receive all benefits of the DASH diet.

Vegetables: 4-5 servings of fresh vegetables such as tomatoes, broccoli, carrots, sweet potatoes and leafy vegetables should be consumed as they are high in vitamin, magnesium, potassium and fibers. In the case of canned vegetables, check the nutritional label and avoid products with added salt.

Fruits: A minimum of 4-5 servings of fruits is recommended to provide necessary fibers and the required energy for the body to carry out daily functions. Fruits could be fresh, dried, frozen or canned. In the case of canned fruits or juices, carefully go through the nutritional label to avoid added sugars. For high quotients of fiber and anti-oxidants try including fruits such as apples, grapefruit and pears. Also try including fruits with low sugar levels. Most fruits have good quantities of magnesium, fiber and potassium and are low in fat.

Dairy: Dairy products such as milk, yogurt and cheese contain protein, calcium, Vitamin D and fat. Aim at a daily serving of 2-3 of low fat or fat free dairy. Dieter may also choose lactose free dairy in case he is intolerant to lactose and have troubles with dairy digestion.

Whole Grains: Recommended consumption of grains is 7-8 servings/day. Whole grains provide more nutrients and fiber than more processed products, so aim at 100% whole-wheat/grain. You can choose from a variety of cereals, pasta and bread; however, avoid topping them with cheese, cream or butter.

Nuts and Seeds: 5-6 servings per week of beans, legumes, seeds and nuts is recommended. They are good sources of phytochemicals, potassium, magnesium, protein and fiber. These nutrients help fight and prevent heart diseases and cancer. Foods in this category especially rich in these nutrients are cashews, almonds, peas, pistachios, peanuts, lentils and kidney beans. As they are also high on calories, one must consume them in small quantities.

Oils and Fats: A minimum of 2-3 servings per day is recommended in the DASH diet. The human body needs fats to absorb nutrients and they also strengthen the immune system. However, the intake should be controlled and limited as they also can lead to cardiovascular disease, diabetes and obesity. One must also be aware of the difference between saturated fat and transfats for better health.

Lean meat, fish and poultry: Up to 6 servings per day of fish, poultry and lean meat is advised. Lean and skinless meat is a source of protein, zinc, iron and B complex vitamins. Fish such as salmon, tuna and herring are recommended as they are rich in Omega 3 fatty acids that can lower cholesterol levels in blood. Try eating them roasted, baked or grilled, but avoid fried.

Alcohol: Recommended for men is not more than two drinks and for women is one drink or less per day. Also limit intake of caffeine as it inflates the blood pressure temporarily.

Sweets: A maximum of 5 servings (or even less if possible) per week is advised. The DASH diet does not require abstaining from sweets totally. However, dieters should keep a check on sweets intake and choose those with lesser fat, such as fruit ices, jelly beans, low-fat cookies and granola bars. Use of artificial sweetener should be curbed, gradually reduced if necessary.

Foods To Avoid On The DASH Diet

In choosing a healthy lifestyle to gain all the benefits the DASH diet offers, a few food items should be avoided. Rejecting foods which have adverse effects should only make sense. Below is a list of such food items:

Sugary beverages

Artificial sweeteners

Salted nuts or seeds

High fat snacks

Dairy with high fat, or whole cream or milk

High sodium salad dressings

In addition, the following should be reduced or eliminated: Red meat

Caffeine

Smoking

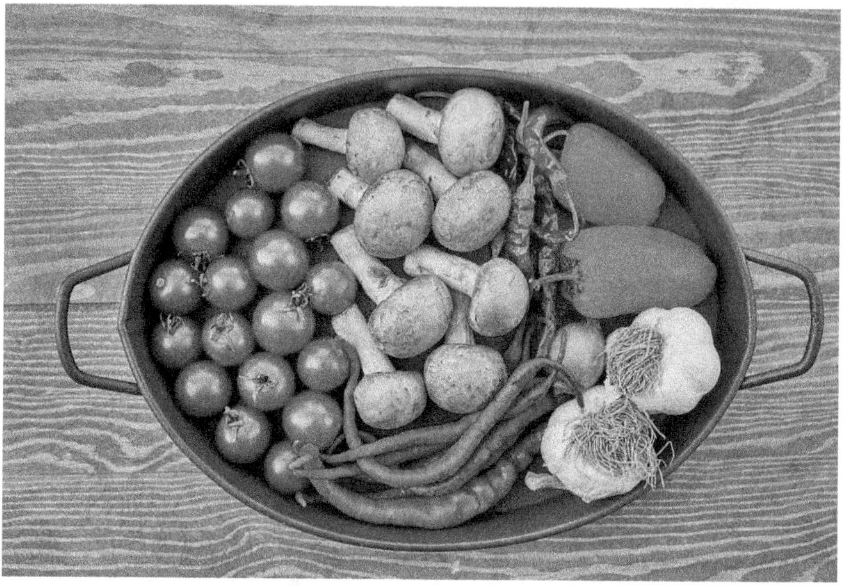

Chapter 8: Basic Shopping List

Following is a list of some of the best DASH approved foods for inclusion in your eating plan. This is not meant to be a set shopping list for each week, but rather a list of suggestions for you to choose from as you plan meals. Extras such as frozen foods and canned goods have not been included in this list. With those foods you should use your discretion and keep in mind your personal dietary goals. There are good options such as frozen fruits and vegetables, frozen whole grain waffles, canned tuna and sugar free applesauce, for example. Prepackaged foods do not need to be avoided altogether, just use good, healthy judgment when choosing them.

Grains and Cereals

Amaranth

Barley

Bran cereal

Buckwheat

Bulgur

Kamut

Low fat granola

Millet

Muesli

Oats, regular or steel cut

Quinoa

Rice, brown

Spelt

Triticale

Tortillas (made from whole wheat or corn)

Wild rice

Whole wheat bagels

Whole wheat bread

Whole wheat couscous

Whole wheat English muffins

Whole wheat pasta

Vegetables

Acorn Squash

Artichokes

Asparagus

Beets

Bell peppers, any color

Broccoli

Brussels sprouts

Butternut squash

Cabbage

Carrots

Cauliflower

Celery

Collard greens

Cucumbers

Eggplant

Green beans

Jicama

Kale

Mushrooms

Leeks

Lettuce

Onions, any color

Parsnips

Peas

Potatoes (limit for weight loss)

Pumpkin

Radishes

Rutabaga

Spaghetti squash

Spinach

Sweet potatoes (limit for weight loss)

Swiss chard

Summer squash

Tomatoes

Turnips

Turnip Greens

Zucchini

Dairy (always choose low fat or fat free options when available)

Buttermilk

Cottage cheese

Fresh cheeses such as feta, fresh mozzarella, queso, etc.

Hard cheeses such as cheddar, Colby, Monterey Jack, Asiago, Parmesan, etc.

Kefir

Margarine, trans fat free varieties

Milk

Ricotta cheese

Soft cheeses, such as blue, gorgonzola, Brie, etc.

Sour cream

Yogurt

Lean Meat, Poultry, and Seafood

Beef, ground (lean)

Beef roast

Beef steak (lean)

Chicken, skinless, preferably light meat pieces

Chicken, ground

Deli meat, low sodium

Eggs

Fresh fish

Pork tenderloin

Shrimp and other seafood

Tempeh

Tofu

Turkey, skinless, preferably light meat pieces

Turkey, ground

Nuts, Seeds, and Legumes

Almonds

Cashews

Dry beans

Hazelnuts

Nut butters

Peanuts

Pecans

Pistachios

Pumpkin seeds

Soy nuts

Sunflower seeds

Walnuts

Condiments

Chili garlic sauce

Dijon mustard

Hot sauce

Hummus

Jams or Jellies, fruit only or sugar free

Marinara sauce, low sodium

Mayonnaise, low fat

Oils, such as olive or canola

Salsa, fresh

Salad dressing, low fat

Soft or liquid margarine trans-fat free

Soy sauce, low sodium

Sun-dried tomatoes

Vinegars, such as apple cider, balsamic, cider, rice wine, red wine, champagne, etc.

Yellow mustard

Suggested Seasonings

Curry powder

Dill

Parsley

Garlic powder

Ginger

Nutmeg

Paprika

Oregano

Pepper:

Rosemary

Sage

Tarragon

Thyme

Variety of Fresh Herbs

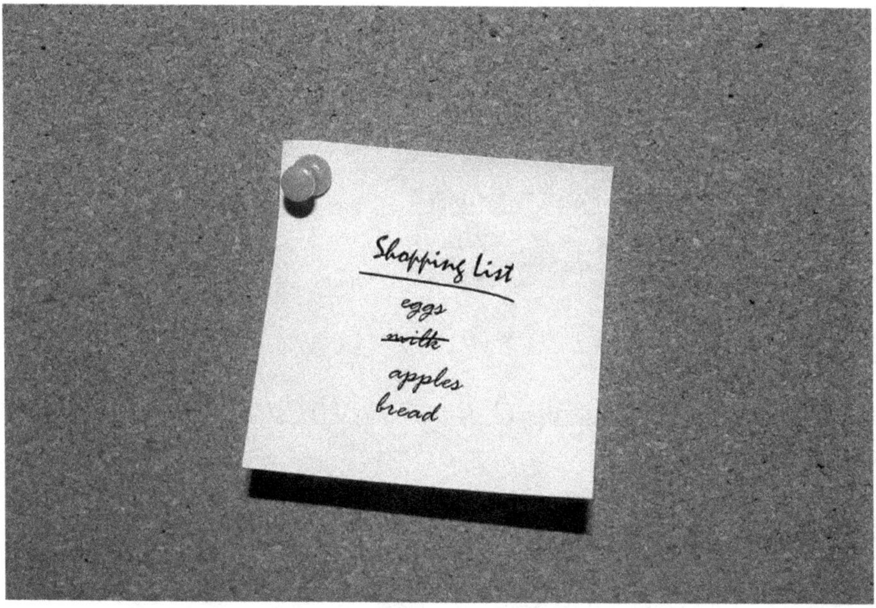
Shopping List
eggs
milk
apples
bread

Chapter 9: A Complete 4 Weeks Diet Meal Plan, day by day

Week 1

Day 1

Breakfast- Whole-grain flax waffles with strawberry purée

Lunch- Vegetable Pasta Soup

Dinner- Chicken Vegetable Bake

Day 2

Breakfast- Spicy baked eggs with goat cheese and spinach

Lunch- Tuna Salad

Dinner- Turkey Fajita Bowls

Day 3

Breakfast- Overnight apple and chia seed refrigerator oatmeal

Lunch- Avocado, Strawberry and Melon Salad

Dinner- Spinach and Quinoa Patties

Day 4

Breakfast- Mushroom and asparagus quinoa frittata

Lunch- Mozzarella Stuffed Portobello Mushroom

Dinner- Spicy Seafood Stew

Day 5

Breakfast- Ricotta toast with tomato and cucumber

Lunch- Noodles with Spinach, Tofu and Mushroom

Dinner- Turkey and Vegetables Stir Fry

Day 6

Breakfast- Pumpkin Granola Yogurt Parfait

Lunch- Shrimp Spring Rolls

Dinner- Shepherd's Pie

Day 7

Breakfast- Superfood green smoothie

Lunch- Chicken Wrap

Dinner- Sweet Pepper Fish and Salsa

Week 2

Day 1

Breakfast- Pineapple-banana high-protein smoothie

Lunch- Savory Millet Cakes

Dinner- Pork Tenderloin with Sweet Potatoes and Apples

Day 2

Breakfast- Buckwheat Crepes

Lunch- Tuna Melt

Dinner- Stuffed Peppers

Day 3

Breakfast- Sweet Potato Oat Waffles

Lunch- Goat Cheese and Red Pepper Frittata

Dinner- Thai Steak Salad

Day 4

Breakfast- French Toast

Lunch- Vegetable Quesadillas with Yoghurt Dips

Dinner- Thai Chicken Pasta Skillet Recipe

Day 5

Breakfast- Open Face Breakfast Sandwich

Lunch- Tuna Melt

Dinner- Lentil Medley

Day 6

Breakfast- Egg and Turkey Bacon Breakfast Tacos

Lunch- Savory Millet Cakes

Dinner- Spiced Salmon

Day 7

Breakfast- Southwest Tofu Scramble

Lunch- Goat Cheese and Red Pepper Frittata

Dinner- Tomato Green Bean Soup

Week 3

Day 1

Breakfast- Spinach Mushroom Omelet

Lunch- Chicken Wrap

Dinner- Citrus Herb Pot Roast

Day 2

Breakfast- Almond Banana Breakfast Smoothie

Lunch- Mozzarella Stuffed Portobello Mushroom

Dinner- Grilled Tilapia and Pineapple Salsa

Day 3

Breakfast- Asparagus Omelet Tortilla Wrap

Lunch- Shrimp Spring Rolls

Dinner- Lentil Medley

Day 4

Breakfast- Raspberry Peach Puff Pancakes

Lunch- Goat Cheese and Red Pepper Frittata

Dinner- Mango Rice Pudding

Day 5

Breakfast- Whole Grain Banana Pancakes

Lunch- Vegetable Quesadillas with Yoghurt Dips

Dinner- Thai-Style Cobb Salad

Day 6

Breakfast- Peanut Butter Overnight Oats

Lunch- Tuna Melt

Dinner- Vegetable and Turkey Barley Soup

Day 7

Breakfast- Muesli Scones

Lunch-Chicken Wrap

Dinner- Grilled Steak Salad

Week 4
Day 1
Breakfast- Apple Cinnamon Oats Cooked Slowly Overnight

Lunch-Vegetable Quesadillas with Yoghurt Dips

Dinner- Garden Vegetable Beef Soup

Day 2
Breakfast- Healthy Breakfast Cookies

Lunch-Vegetable Quesadillas with Yoghurt Dips

Dinner- Asparagus Soup

Day 3
Breakfast- Sweet Potato Oat Waffles

Lunch- Goat Cheese and Red Pepper Frittata

Dinner- Thai Steak Salad

Day 4
Breakfast- French Toast

Lunch- Vegetable Quesadillas with Yoghurt Dips

Dinner- Thai Chicken Pasta Skillet Recipe

Day 5

Breakfast- Open Face Breakfast Sandwich

Lunch- Tuna Melt

Dinner- Lentil Medley

Day 6

Breakfast- Egg and Turkey Bacon Breakfast Tacos

Lunch- Savory Millet Cakes

Dinner- Spiced Salmon

Day 7

Breakfast- Southwest Tofu Scramble

Lunch- Goat Cheese and Red Pepper Frittata

Dinner- Tomato Green Bean Soup

Chapter 10: Breakfast Dash Recipes

Whole-grain flax waffles with strawberry purée

Total time: 30 minutes

Ingredients

For the strawberry purée

- 1 quart fresh strawberries, hulled and chopped
- 1 cup water
- 2 tablespoons honey
- ½ teaspoon vanilla extract

For the waffles

- 2 ¼ cups whole-wheat flour or whole-wheat pastry flour
- ¼ cup ground flaxseed
- 2 ½ teaspoons baking powder
- 1 teaspoon baking soda
- ½ teaspoon kosher salt
- ¼ cup canola oil
- 2 tablespoons dark brown sugar

- 2 teaspoons ground cinnamon
- 3 large eggs
- 2 teaspoons vanilla extract
- 1 cup nonfat milk
- Nonstick cooking spray, for cooking the waffles

Directions for strawberry purée

In a medium saucepan over medium heat, combine the strawberries, water, honey, and vanilla. Bring to a simmer and cook for 5 to 6 minutes until the strawberries are soft. Use an immersion blender to purée the strawberries in the saucepan, or transfer the mixture to a blender and purée until smooth.

Directions for the waffles

1. In a medium bowl, whisk the flour, flaxseed, baking powder, baking soda, and salt until combined. Set the dry ingredients aside.

2. In a large bowl, whisk the canola oil, brown sugar, and cinnamon until well combined.

3. One at a time, whisk in the eggs until the mixture is fluffy.

4. Add the vanilla and milk, and whisk until combined.

5. Slowly whisk the dry ingredients into the wet ingredients.

6. Heat a Belgian waffle maker over medium heat. Once hot, coat with the cooking spray. Evenly spoon ⅔ cup of the batter into the waffle maker. Close the lid and cook for 1½ to 2 minutes until the waffle is browned on the outside. Repeat with the remaining batter.

7. Serve the waffles with the strawberry purée.

8. Once cooled, you can refrigerate the waffles in an airtight container or sealed plastic bag for up to five days. Serve chilled, or reheat in the microwave on high power for 30 seconds. Refrigerate the strawberry purée in a separate airtight container for up to five days.

Spicy baked eggs with goat cheese and spinach

Total time: 25 minutes

Ingredients

- Nonstick cooking spray, for preparing the ramekins
- 10 ounces frozen chopped spinach, thawed and squeezed dry
- 4 large eggs
- ¼ cup chunky salsa
- ¼ cup crumbled goat cheese
- Freshly ground black pepper

Directions

1. Preheat the oven to 325°F. Spray four (6-ounce) ramekins with cooking spray.

2. Cover the bottom of each ramekin with spinach. Make a slight indentation in the center of the spinach in each ramekin and crack an egg into it.

3. Top each egg with 1 tablespoon of salsa and 1 tablespoon of goat cheese. Season with pepper.

4. Place the ramekins on a baking sheet and bake for about 20 minutes, or until the whites are completely set but the yolks are still a bit runny. Serve immediately.

Overnight apple and chia seed refrigerator oatmeal

Total time: 5 minutes

Ingredients

- ½ cup low-fat milk
- ½ cup low-fat plain Greek yogurt
- ¼ cup unsweetened applesauce
- ¼ cup old-fashioned rolled oats
- 1 ½ teaspoons chia seeds

- ⅛ teaspoon ground cinnamon

Directions

1. In a half-pint Mason jar, or any small container fitted with a lid, combine the milk, yogurt, applesauce, oats, chia seeds, and cinnamon.

2. Cover the jar and shake until well until combined. Refrigerate overnight and eat chilled the next day.

Mushroom and asparagus quinoa frittata

Total time: 40 minutes

Ingredients

- 2 teaspoons extra-virgin olive oil
- 1 ½ cups sliced mushrooms
- 1 ½ cups (1-inch) asparagus pieces
- ¼ teaspoon kosher salt, divided
- 1 cup chopped tomato
- 8 large eggs
- 4 large egg whites
- ½ cup low-fat milk
- ⅛ teaspoon freshly ground black pepper

- 1 cup cooked quinoa

- ½ cup shredded part-skim mozzarella cheese

Directions

1. Preheat the oven to 350°F and set the oven rack to the middle position.

2. In a medium oven-safe skillet or sauté pan, heat the olive oil over medium heat for 1 minute.

3. Add the mushrooms, asparagus, and ⅛ teaspoon of salt. Sauté for 5 to 6 minutes until the mushrooms are lightly browned and have released their moisture.

4. Add the tomato and cook 3 minutes more. Remove from the heat.

5. In a medium bowl, whisk the eggs, egg whites, milk, the remaining ⅛ teaspoon of salt, and the pepper.

6. Add the quinoa and cheese and stir until well combined. Add the egg mixture to the vegetables, gently stirring with a wooden spoon so the vegetables are evenly distributed.

7. Place the skillet on the middle rack and cook for 20 minutes, or until the egg mixture has set.

Ricotta toast with tomato and cucumber

Total time: 10 minutes

Ingredients

- ½ cup part-skim ricotta
- 1 tablespoon finely chopped scallion
- ¼ teaspoon Salt-Free Italian Seasoning
- ⅛ teaspoon freshly ground black pepper
- 1 slice whole-grain or whole-wheat bread, toasted
- 1 small tomato, thinly sliced
- ¼ English cucumber, thinly sliced

1. In a small mixing bowl, combine the ricotta, scallion, Italian seasoning, and pepper. Using a rubber spatula, gently mix the ingredients to combine.

2. To assemble, spread the toast with the ricotta mixture and top with the tomato and cucumber slices. Serve immediately.

Superfood green smoothie

Total time: 10 minutes

Ingredients

- 1 cup coarsely chopped kale leaves
- 1 cup fresh spinach leaves

- 1 medium Hass avocado, pitted and coarsely chopped
- ½ medium apple, peeled and coarsely chopped
- ½ to ¾ cup cold water
- 2 tablespoons freshly squeezed lemon
- 2 or 3 ice cubes

Directions

1. In a blender, combine the kale, spinach, avocado, and apple and process until smooth.

2. Slowly add the water, lemon juice, and ice and pulse until puréed. Serve immediately.

PREPARATION TIP: Change the amount of water and ice to suit how thick or thin you prefer your smoothies. For a thinner smoothie, add more water and less ice. For a thicker smoothie, you can decrease the amount of water and increase the amount of ice.

Pineapple-banana high-protein smoothie

Total time: 10 minutes

Ingredients

- ½ cup fresh or frozen pineapple cubes
- ½ medium banana

- ½ cup low-fat plain Greek yogurt

- ¼ medium Hass avocado, peeled, pitted, and coarsely chopped

- ½ to ¾ cup low-fat milk

- 2 or 3 ice cubes

Directions

1. In a blender, combine the pineapple, banana, yogurt, and avocado. Process until smooth.

2. Slowly add the milk and ice and pulse until puréed. Serve immediately.

Buckwheat Crepes

Total time: 20 minutes

Ingredients

- 2 ¼ cups buckwheat flour (300g)

- 750 ml of water (3 cups)

- 1 egg (flax-egg, if vegan)

- Butter or coconut oil

- ½ tsp. salt

- Shallots, mushrooms, garlic, nutmeg, and oregano (optional)

Directions

1. Add the buckwheat flour, egg, water, and salt to a blender and mix it until smooth. You can also use a mixing bowl if you do not have a blender.

2. Cover this batter and let it sit in the refrigerator overnight or for at least 2 hours.

3. When you take out the mixture, make sure the consistency resembles that of melted ice cream.

4. Heat the crepe pan and grease it with ¼ tsp. butter or coconut oil.

5. Pour ⅓ cup batter into the pan and spread it thinly by rotating the pan.

6. Keep flipping both sides for 1 to 2 minutes to brown it up. Repeat the process.

7. Stir-fry the shallots, mushrooms, garlic, and nutmeg with oregano and put it inside the crepes.

Pumpkin Granola Yogurt Parfait

Total time: 2 hours 50 minutes

Ingredients

- 5 cups rolled oats; if you want to add nuts, add 3 cups oats and 1 cup nuts
- ½ tsp. salt
- 1 ½ tsp. pumpkin pie spice
- 1 ½ tsp. cinnamon
- ¼ cup brown sugar
- ½ cup honey
- 2 tsp. vanilla
- ⅓ cup coconut oil
- Light pumpkin pie yogurt
- 3 tbsp. canned pumpkin

Directions

1. Mix the pumpkin puree, oats, spice, honey, vanilla, maple syrup, and cinnamon in a bowl.

2. Heat a pan for about 15 minutes and then add the mixture to the pan.

3. Bake the mixture until it is golden brown in color. Bake in 15-minutes intervals and stir at every interval.

4. Allow it to cool completely. You may even freeze it as well. When you cool the food, it becomes even tastier. This is a fantastic way to serve this recipe.

*5.*Serve it with yogurt and granola layers. Enjoy.

Sweet Potato Oat Waffles

Total time: 15 minutes

Ingredients

- 1 cooked large sweet potato
- ½ cup flour
- ½ cup oats
- 2 eggs
- ½ cup almond milk
- ¾ tsp. cinnamon
- 1 tsp. baking powder
- ¼ tsp. salt
- Cooking spray

Directions

*1.*Set the waffle maker to preheat before you start making the waffles.

*2.*Take a jar for blending and add all the ingredients to it. The process is as instructed here. After that, wait until the mixture is blended and forms a puree.

3. Set the batter aside for about 10 minutes, as this will give you the best results. Letting it rest will give it a nutty, sweet potato flavor.

4. Pour the batter into the mold. Make sure the batter fills about ⅓ of the mold to make the perfect waffle.

5. When the indicator on the waffle iron turns green, cook the waffles for an additional 30 seconds. You can cook them for 4 to 5 minutes per batch.

6. Serve the waffles with maple syrup, whipped cream, pecans, or anything else as desired.

French Toast

Total time: 16 minutes

Ingredients

- 2 large eggs
- 1 large egg white
- ½ cup 2% milk
- 1 tbsp. butter, melted
- 1 tbsp. honey
- 1 tbsp. sugar
- ½ tsp. ground cinnamon
- ¼ tsp. salt

- Nonstick cooking spray
- ¼ tsp. vanilla extract
- 8 slices of light bread

Directions

1. In a wide mixing bowl, add egg white, milk, sugar, butter, honey, and vanilla extract along with salt. Whip using a whipper.

2. On a non-stick skillet or large griddle, spray some nonstick cooking spray and keep it on a low flame.

3. Dip the pieces of bread into the mixing bowl and place them on the skillet. Ensure that you have coated both sides of the bread with the mixture. You can place as much bread on the skillet as you want, but make sure they fit properly without overlapping each other.

4. Fry the bread over a medium flame until it is golden brown. Fry at least 3 minutes or more if required.

5. Serve the French toast hot and garnish with fresh berries. You can also pour pure maple syrup on top of the bread to enhance the taste.

Open Face Breakfast Sandwich

Total time: 15 minutes

Ingredients

- 2 slices of bread
- 4 rashers of bacon
- 2 eggs
- 1 tbsp. milk
- ½ sliced tomato
- Four heaping tbsp. guacamole: ½ sliced avocado, ½ mashed avocado
- Pepper to taste
- Cilantro for garnish

Directions

1. Toast the slices of bread in an oven or toaster until they are crisp and brown.

2. Cook the bacon over medium heat and drain the excess oil using paper towels. Once it is cooled, chop the bacon into small pieces.

3. In another bowl, whisk the eggs and the milk together. Fry the eggs sunny side up and add salt and pepper as per taste.

4. Spread avocado on the bread slices

5. Top with the eggs and add diced tomatoes on top.

6. You can add cilantro for a garnish along with the chopped bacon.

*7.*Your sandwich is ready. Serve it hot for breakfast and get ready for the day with delicious food.

Egg and Turkey Bacon Breakfast Tacos

Total time: 30 minutes

Ingredients

- 1 large egg
- 3 large egg whites
- A bit of almond milk
- Salt and pepper to taste
- 4 pieces of turkey or regular bacon
- 2 tbsp. shredded cheddar cheese
- ½ cup halved cherry tomatoes
- ½ cubed avocado
- 4 white corn tortillas (taco-sized)

Directions

*1.*Preheat the oven to 400ºF. Line a baking sheet with tin foil.

*2.*Place the 4 strips of turkey bacon on the sheet and bake it for around 15 minutes. You can even bake it for a couple minutes longer if you want it to be crispier.

3. Once they are baked, set the turkey bacon strips aside and whisk together 1 egg and 3 egg whites, along with some almond milk in a small bowl.

4. Spray coconut oil on a nonstick pan and heat to medium/high heat.

5. Grab a spatula and scramble the eggs along with some salt and pepper seasoning.

6. Spread the scrambled eggs on 4 tortillas. Put a bacon strip on each.

7. Top it with cherry tomatoes, avocado, cheese, and cilantro.

Southwest Tofu Scramble

Total time: 30 minutes

Ingredients

- 1 lb. extra-firm tofu, drained
- ¼ cup nutritional yeast
- 3 garlic cloves, minced
- 1 red bell pepper, finely chopped
- 3 tbsp. water
- 2 tsp. ground cumin
- 1 tsp. dried thyme, crushed with your fingers

- ½ tsp. ground turmeric
- Ground black pepper to taste

Directions

1.Take a small bowl and add some thyme, cumin, and turmeric. Pour some water and mix it into a thick solution. Set it aside.

2.Take a large, heavy-bottomed pan and preheat it over a medium flame.

3.Take the tofu and break into small pieces. Sauté the pieces for around 10 minutes with a spatula. Keep stirring it. Cook the tofu until it is light brown on one side and until the water in the pan has evaporated.

4.Add the garlic and red pepper to the pan and cook it for 5 minutes.

5.Add the blended spices and mix them together.

6.Add the fresh black pepper and nutritional yeast.

7.Cook the whole thing for another 5 minutes and serve when it's warm.

Spinach Mushroom Omelet

Total time: 30 minutes

Ingredients

- 1 egg
- 3 egg whites
- 1 tbsp. grated Parmesan cheese
- 1 tbsp. shredded cheddar cheese
- ¼ tsp. salt
- ⅛ tsp. crushed red pepper flakes
- ⅛ tsp. garlic powder
- ⅛ tsp. pepper
- ½ cup sliced fresh mushrooms
- 2 tbsp. finely chopped green pepper
- 1 tbsp. finely chopped onion
- ½ tsp. olive oil
- 1 cup torn fresh spinach

Directions

1. Take a small bowl and beat the egg whites and the eggs using a whipper. Add the salt, cheese, garlic powder, and pepper flakes. Set it aside after mixing it well.

2. Take an 8-inch nonstick skillet and add the mushrooms, onion, green pepper, and oil. Sauté them until they appear to be tender. Add the spinach and keep stirring until they are wilted. Add the egg mixture. When the egg mixture appears to be set, lift its edges and let the uncooked part get underneath it

3. Your spinach mushroom omelet is ready to be served. You can serve the spinach mushroom omelet by cutting it into small pieces while it is still hot.

Almond Banana Breakfast Smoothie

Total time: 10 minutes

Ingredients

- 2 pieces of big, ripe, peeled and sliced bananas
- 2 cups whole milk or almond milk
- 2 cups ice cubes
- 2 tbsp. packed brown sugar
- 1 heaping tsp. vanilla extract

Directions

1. Take a blender and add the slices of banana.

2. Add your choice of milk.

3. Add 2 heaping spoons of brown sugar.

4. Add the vanilla extract.

5. Turn on the blender and let the mixture blend until it forms a thick liquid.

6. Make sure no chunks of banana are left in the smoothie.

7. Top it with ice cubes before serving.

Asparagus Omelet Tortilla Wrap

Total time: 20 minutes

Ingredients

- 1 large egg
- 1 large egg whites
- 1 tbsp. fat-free milk
- 2 tsp. Parmesan cheese, grated
- ⅛ tsp. pepper
- 4 fresh asparagus spears, trimmed and sliced
- 1 tsp. butter
- 1 chopped green onion
- 1 whole-wheat 8-inch tortilla, warmed

Directions

1.Take a small bowl and add the first 5 ingredients. Whisk them continuously until they blend. Then, place them in a small nonstick skillet. Spray it with cooking oil over medium heat. Add the asparagus and stir continuously for 3 to 4 minutes until it is crispy tender.

2.Remove the asparagus from the pan and set it aside. In the same pan, add some butter and heat it over a medium flame. Pour the mixture of egg on it. As the edges of the egg mixture set on the edges of the pan, start pushing the cooked part of the mixture towards the center of the eggs. Let the uncooked part of the eggs get underneath it. Let the eggs thicken and make sure no liquid portion is left. Put some green onions and asparagus on one side of the omelet.

3.Fold the omelet in half and serve it in the tortilla.

Raspberry Peach Puff Pancakes

Total time: 35 minutes

Ingredients

- 2 medium peaches, peeled and sliced
- ½ cup fresh raspberries
- 1 tbsp. butter
- ½ cup all-purpose flour
- 3 large eggs, lightly beaten

- ½ cup fat-free milk
- ½ tsp. sugar
- ⅛ tsp. salt
- ¼ cup vanilla yogurt

Directions

1. Preheat the oven to 400°. Put some peaches, raspberries, and sugar in a small bowl and start stirring.

2. Once properly stirred, place the butter in a 9-inch pie plate and heat it in the oven until the butter is melted.

3. In the meantime, whisk some eggs, milk, and salt until blended and whisk it in flour. After removing the pie plate from the oven, carefully tilt it to coat the sides and the bottom.

4. With the butter settling in the bowl, pour in the egg mixture immediately.

5. Bake it until the pancake is brown and puffed, which should take about 15-20 minutes. Serve it immediately.

6. You can accentuate its taste by adding fruit and yogurt to the plating.

Whole Grain Banana Pancakes

Total time: 30 minutes

Ingredients

- 1 ⅓ cups whole wheat flour
- 2 tsp. baking powder
- ¼ tsp. salt
- 1 tsp. ground cinnamon
- 2 egg whites
- 1 cup milk
- ½ cup mashed ripe banana
- 2 tbsp. packed light or dark brown sugar
- 1 tsp. vanilla extract
- ¼ cup Greek yogurt
- ½ cup add-ins like fruit or chocolate chips

Directions

1. Keep aside the salt, flour, baking powder, and cinnamon in a bowl. Whisk the milk, egg, and banana in brown sugar and yogurt until there are no lumps. Add the vanilla until it is thoroughly combined.

2. Once done, make a well in the dry ingredients and fill it with the wet ingredients. Without overmixing it, stir until it is combined and the mixture is tight and dense. To this, add any mix-ins you like, but don't overmix it.

3. Preheat the skittle over medium heat and coat it with oil or butter. Once it's appropriately heated, drop a quarter of the batter on the grill and cook it until the edges start to look dry and bubbles begin to form.

4. Once done, flip it over and cook 2 more minutes.

5. Keep the pancakes warm until they are cooked all the way. Serve immediately.

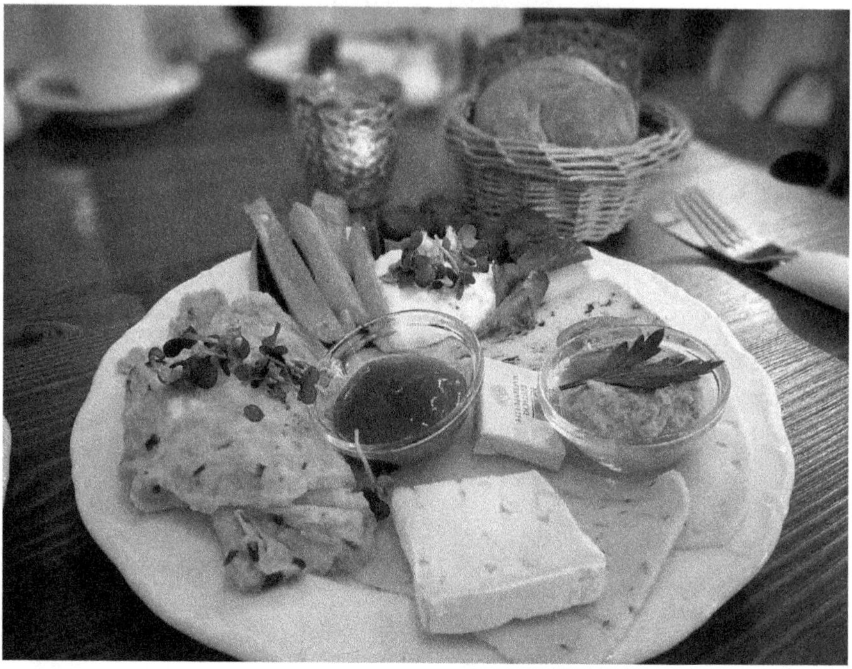

Chapter 11: Lunch Dash Recipes

Vegetable Pasta Soup

Total time: 20 minutes

Ingredients

- 2 tsp olive oil
- 6 cloves garlic (peeled, washed and minced)
- 2 cups Carrot (peeled, washed and shredded)
- 2 large onions (peeled and finely chopped)
- 3 stalks celery (finely sliced)
- 2 1/2 cups chicken broth (low-sodium)
- 3 cups water
- 2 cups Pasta

  <u>For toppings</u>

- 1 cup Parmesan Cheese (grated)
- 2 tbsp fresh parsley

Directions:

1. Place a Dutch oven over medium heat and add oil to it. When the oil is warm, add garlic to the oven and cook until the garlic turns golden brown and is fragrant.

2. Now, add the finely chopped onions to the oven and cook until the onions are tender and golden brown.

3. Add celery and carrot to the oven and stir until they are soft.

4. Add the broth and water to the oven and bring the ingredients in the oven to a boil. Now, add paste to the oven and cover and cook until the pasta is tender.

5. Drain the liquid from the oven and transfer the pasta and vegetables into a serving dish.

6. Top with Parmesan cheese and parsley and serve hot.

Tuna Salad

Total time: 15 minutes

Ingredients

- 2 14 oz. cans of tuna (drained)
- 1 12 oz. can of white beans (drained and rinsed)
- 12 cherry tomatoes (washed and quartered)
- 8 scallions (trimmed and sliced)

- 2 tbsp Extra Virgin Olive oil
- 2 tbsp lemon juice
- 1/4 tsp salt
- Ground pepper to taste

Directions:

1. Combine all the ingredients in a large mixing bowl and stir well.

2. Toss the ingredients until the salad is well balanced.

3. Cover the bowl and leave in the refrigerator for two hours.

4. Serve it cold.

Avocado, Strawberry and Melon Salad

Total time: 20 minutes

Ingredients

- 1/2 cup honey
- 2 tbsp vinegar (red wine or sherry vinegar)
- 2 tbsp mint (chopped)
- 1/4 tsp freshly ground pepper

- 1/4 tsp salt

- 3 cups spinach

- 1 small avocado (pitted, cored and sliced)

- 20 thin slices of cantaloupe (remove the rind)

- 2 cups strawberries (finely sliced)

- 2 tsp sesame seeds (preferably roasted)

Directions:

1. Combine the vinegar, mint, honey, salt and pepper in a bowl and whisk until they are well combined. Adjust the seasoning if necessary.

2. Transfer the spinach to a large salad bowl and arrange the avocado and cantaloupe slices in the bowls. Alternate between the two fruit.

3. Top the fruit with sesame seeds and strawberry slices.

4. Pour the dressing over the salad ingredients and toss until the fruit are coated well with the dressing.

5. Refrigerate the plates and serve them cold!

Mozzarella Stuffed Portobello Mushroom

Total time: 40 minutes

Ingredients

- 3 Portobello mushrooms cups (cleaned and destemmed)
- 2 small tomatoes (diced)
- 3 tbsp pesto
- 1/2 cup low-fat mozzarella cheese (shredded)

Directions:

1. Preheat the oven to 150 degrees Fahrenheit.

2. Divide the pesto equally between the three mushroom cups.

3. Top the pesto with the diced tomato and shredded cheese.

4. Bake for thirty minutes.

Noodles with Spinach, Tofu and Mushroom

Total time: 30 minutes

Ingredients

- 2 tbsp canola oil
- 1 shallot (Minced)

- 3 carrots (Diced finely)
- 2 cloves garlic (peeled, washed and minced)
- 2 tbsp fresh ginger (Minced)
- 6 ounces brown or white mushrooms (washed, destemmed and finely sliced)
- 1 1/2 cups thawed edamame
- 2 1/2 cups low-sodium vegetable broth
- 2 tbsp low sodium soy sauce
- 1 tsp grated lemon zest
- 3 ounces spinach leaves (finely chopped)
- 2 ounces tofu (cubed)
- ½ tsp ground pepper
- 5 ounces soba noodles

For the garnish

- 1/2 cup parmesan cheese (shredded)

Directions:

*1.*Place a 6-quart pot on high heat and add water to it. Bring the water to a boil.

2. While the water is boiling, place a saucepan over medium heat and add canola oil to it. When the oil is warm, add the shallots and garlic to the pan.

3. Cook until the shallots and garlic turn golden brown.

4. Add carrots and ginger to the pan and sauté for a few more minutes.

5. Now, add the mushroom slices to the pan and stir. Cover the pan and cook until the mushroom slices have released their juices and are soft.

6. Uncover the pan and increase the heat.

7. Add edamame to the pan and sauté until the ingredients are well cooked.

8. Combine the broth, lemon zest and the soy sauce in a small bowl and add them to the pan. Bring all the liquid in the pan to a boil.

9. Add the spinach little by little and stir the ingredients in the pan until the spinach has wilted. Now, add the tofu cubes to the pan and turn off the heat. Season the ingredients in the pan with pepper.

10. If the water in the pot has come to a boil, add the noodles and a pinch of salt to the pot. Cook until the noodles are tender to touch. When the noodles have cooked well, you will need to drain the water out of the pan and remove any excess water.

11. Add the noodles to the pan and turn the heat to medium flame.

12. Toss the noodles with the mixture in the pan until the noodles have been cooked through and divide the noodles into six pasta bowls and serve hot.

13. Garnish with shredded Parmesan cheese and serve.

Shrimp Spring Rolls

Total time: 40 minutes

Ingredients

- 6 sheets rice paper
- 6 bibb lettuce leaves
- 6 basil leaves
- 1/2 cup fresh cilantro
- 1/2 cup carrots (shredded)
- 1 medium cucumber (thinly sliced)
- 1-pound shrimp (washed, peeled and deveined)
- 1 tbsp olive oil

Directions:

1.Place a non-stick skillet over medium heat and add olive oil to it. When the oil is warm, add the shrimp to the skillet and cook until the shrimp turn golden.

Remove the skillet from heat and set aside.

2.Lay a damp paper towel on a cutting board or the counter. Wash the rice paper with warm water and place it on the paper towel.

3.Place one lettuce leaf, one basil leaf, one tablespoon cilantro, carrot and cucumber on the rice paper and begin to roll the paper carefully over the vegetables.

4.When the vegetables are covered with the rice paper, add the shrimp to the paper and continue to roll like a burrito. Tuck the ends of the wrap.

5.Repeat the process until the 6 rolls are made.

6.Serve immediately.

Chicken Wrap

Total time: 50 minutes

Ingredients

- 1 large chicken breast (8 ounces)
- 1/2 cup canned mandarins (drain the juice)

- 1 cup celery, coarsely chopped

- 1/2 cup onions (minced)

- 3 tbsp mayonnaise

- 2 tsp soy sauce

- 1/2 tsp garlic powder

- 1/2 tsp black pepper

- 1 whole wheat tortilla

- 2 large lettuce leaves

Directions:

*1.*Place a non-stick skillet on medium heat and cook the chicken breast until it is fully cooked (the internal temperature will need to be 165 degrees Fahrenheit).

Leave the chicken to cool to room temperature and cut into half-inch cubes.

*2.*Add celery, oranges, onions and chicken cubes to a bowl and stir them together. Add soy sauce, mayonnaise, pepper and garlic to the bowl and stir until the chicken cubes are coated well.

*3.*Place the whole-wheat tortilla on a large plate and cut the tortilla into quarters.

*4.*Place one lettuce leaf on a tortilla quarter.

5. Add the chicken mix to the tortilla quarter and roll them up.

6. Serve the wraps with a dip of your choice.

Savory Millet Cakes

Total time: 40 minutes

Ingredients

- 2 tbsp extra virgin olive oil
- ½ cup chopped onion (finely chopped)
- 2 cups millets
- 2 cloves garlic (peeled, washed and minced)
- 5 cups water
- 1 tsp coarse salt
- 1 cup shredded zucchini (peeled and shredded)
- 1 cup shredded carrot (peeled and shredded)
- 1 cup shredded Parmesan cheese
- 3 tsp fresh thyme
- 2 tsp lemon zest (fresh)

- ½ tsp ground pepper

- 1 small cup low-fat sour cream

- Cooking spray

Directions:

*1.*Place a large saucepan on medium flame. When it is hot, add the oil to the pan.

*2.*When the oil has warmed, add the onions to the pan and cook until the onions have turned golden brown and are transparent.

*3.*Now, add the garlic to the pan and cook until you get the fragrance of the garlic. Next, add the salt and the water to the pan and let ingredients boil.

*4.*When the water boils, lower the flame and put a lid on the pan. Continue to cook the ingredients for another five minutes and stir every two minutes.

*5.*Now, add the zucchini and carrot to the pan and cook until the vegetables become soft.

*6.*Now, add lemon zest, pepper and thyme to the pan and stir. Cover the pan and cook for another two minutes.

*7.*Uncover the pan and continue to stir the ingredients to ensure that the millets do not stick to the bottom of the pan.

8. When the mixture is thick and soft, remove the pan off the heat and stir the ingredients until the pan is cool.

9. Wet your hands a little bit and start shaping the millet mixture into patties or cakes depending on how you like it. Make sure that you make a 4-inch diameter.

10. Place a non-stick skillet on the gas and spray it with cooking spray. Turn the heat to medium and add four of the cakes to the skillet and cook them all in batches. You will need to cook until both the sides of the cake have turned brown and the cake has been cooked through fully.

11. Cook all the cakes one more time to ensure that they are fully cooked through.

Serve hot with a low-fat sour cream dip.

Tuna Melt

Total time: 20 minutes

Ingredients

- 3 ounces white tuna packed in water (drained)
- 2 onions, minced
- 1/2 cup celery

- 1/2 cup low-fat Thousand Island or Russian Salad Dressing

- 3 whole-wheat English muffins (split)

- 4 ounces low-fat Cheddar cheese (grated)

- Salt and black pepper, as per taste

Directions:

1. Preheat the broiler.

2. Combine the salad dressing, onion and tuna in a bowl and toss the tuna to ensure that it is coated well with the dressing. Sprinkle salt and pepper and toss the ingredients one more time.

3. Toast the English muffin halves and place them on a baking sheet. Top each half with a portion of the tuna mixture.

4. Broil for five minutes or until the tuna is heated through.

5. Top the muffins with cheese and broil until the cheese is melted.

6. Serve hot.

Goat Cheese and Red Pepper Frittata

Total time: 40 minutes

Ingredients

- 6 eggs

- 2 tbsp oregano (fresh and finely chopped)

- 1/2 tsp salt

- 1/4 tsp ground pepper

- 2 tbsp extra virgin olive oil

- 1 cup finely sliced red bell pepper

- 2 bunches scallions (trimmed and sliced)

- 1 cup goat cheese (shredded or crumbled)

Directions:

1. Preheat the oven to 200 degrees Fahrenheit and place a rack in the upper third area of the oven.

2. Crack the eggs in a medium-sized bowl and whisk them well until you obtain a fluffy mixture.

3. Add the salt, pepper and oregano to the bowl and mix the ingredients well together.

4.Place a large pan over medium heat and add oil to it. When the oil is hot, add scallions and red bell peppers to the pan and cook until scallions are tender.

5.Pour the egg mixture over the vegetables and cook until the egg has set.

6.Flip the frittata and ensure that both sides are fully cooked. Cook until both sides of the frittata are golden brown.

7.Add the cheese to the frittata and place the pan on the rack in the oven. Bake, the frittata for ten minutes or until the top is puffy and golden.

8.Leave the frittata to cool for five minutes and serve warm.

Vegetable Quesadillas with Yoghurt Dips

Total time: 20 minutes

Ingredients

- 2 cups beans

- 3 tbsp cilantro (chopped)

- 1 bell pepper (finely chopped)

- 1 cup corn kernels

- 2 cups low-fat parmesan cheese (shredded)
- 8 corn tortillas
- 2 medium carrots (shredded)
- 1 jalapeno pepper (finely minced)

For the Yoghurt Dip

- 2 cups plain non-fat yogurt
- 3 tbsp cilantro (finely chopped)
- 1 tsp lime juice (fresh)

Directions:

1. Place a large skillet over medium heat.

2. Place four tortillas on the counter and divide the corn, cheese, beans, shredded carrots, peppers and cilantro among them.

3. Cover each tortilla with another tortilla and set aside.

4. Place each tortilla roll on the skillet and cook until the cheese has melted and the tortilla is golden brown.

5. Flip and cook the roll on the other side until it turns golden brown.

6. Repeat the process with the remaining tortilla rolls.

7.Combine the ingredients for the yogurt dip in a small bowl and whisk until the ingredients are well combined.

8.Serve the quesadilla hot with the dip.

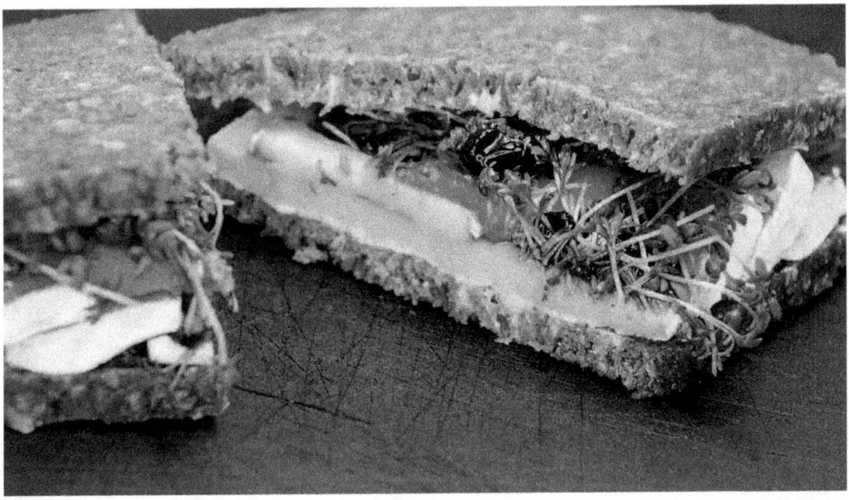

Chapter 12: Dinner Dash Recipes

Chicken Vegetable Bake

Total time: 55 minutes

Ingredients

- 2 cups sliced mushrooms (washed and de-stemmed)
- 1 cup yellow and red bell pepper (Alternatively you can choose sweet peppers)
- 1 onion (finely chopped)
- 2 cloves garlic (peel, wash and mince)
- 2 tbsp olive oil
- 1/4 cup all-purpose flour
- 1 tsp salt
- 1/2 tsp dried thyme (crushed)
- 1/4 tsp black pepper
- 1 1/2 cups low-fat or fat-free milk
- 1 cup chopped spinach
- 1 1/2 cups cooked white or brown rice
- 2 cups chopped chicken

- 1/2 cup shredded Parmesan cheese

Directions:

*1.*Preheat the oven to 200 degrees Fahrenheit.

*2.*Place a skillet on medium heat and add olive oil to it, add onions and garlic to the skillet. Cook the ingredients until the onions have turned golden brown and soft.

*3.*Now, add the mushroom slices and mixed peppers to the skillet and cook until the mushrooms have released their juices. Continue to cook until the mushroom slices are soft.

*4.*Add the thyme, flour, salt and black pepper. Stir the ingredients well until the mixture is well balanced. Adjust the seasoning if necessary.

*5.*Pour the milk slowly into the skillet while continuously stirring. Bring the ingredients in the skillet to a boil.

*6.*Now, add the chicken, spinach and rice to the skillet and stir well. Stir the ingredients until the chopped chicken is coated well with the sauce.

*7.*Add the cheese to the skillet and continue to cook until the cheese has melted.

*8.*Coat the insides of a baking dish with cooking spray and transfer the mixture in the skillet into the dish.

9. Cover the dish and bake for fifteen minutes while it is covered. Then uncover the dish and bake for five more minutes or until the dish is fully cooked.

10. Serve hot.

Turkey Fajita Bowls

Total time: 40 minutes

Ingredients

- 1-pound turkey breast
- 3 tbsp olive oil
- 2 tbsp lemon juice
- 2 cloves garlic (peeled, washed and crushed)
- 1 tsp fresh chile pepper (dried)
- 1 tsp oregano leaves (dried)
- 1 cup mixed peppers (cut into 1-inch pieces)
- 2 medium tomatoes (cut into wedges)
- 6 corn tortillas

For topping

- 1 cup cheddar cheese (shredded)
- 5 tbsp salsa

Directions:

1.Cut turkey into strips and lay them out on a plate.

2.Combine lemon juice, garlic, chile pepper, oregano and one tablespoon of olive oil in a bowl and whisk until well combined. Adjust the seasoning if necessary.

3.Coat the turkey strips with the dressing and leave the strips to marinate for half an hour.

4.Place a non-stick skillet over medium heat and add the remaining olive oil to it. When the oil is warm, add the mixed peppers to the skillet and cook for two minutes.

5.Add the turkey strips to the skillet and cook for two minutes before adding the tomato.

6.Warm the tortillas in a separate skillet and add the turkey filling.

7.Top with salsa and cheese and serve.

Spinach and Quinoa Patties

Total time: 30 minutes

Ingredients

- 2 cups uncooked quinoa
- 5 eggs (lightly beaten)

- 1/2 cup parmesan cheese
- 4 large scallions (thinly sliced)
- 3 cloves garlic (peeled, washed and minced)
- 2 cups spinach (steamed and chopped)
- 2 cups whole wheat breadcrumbs
- 2 tsp olive oil
- 3 cups water

Directions:

1. Place a saucepan over medium heat and add water to it. Bring the water to a boil.

2. Rinse the quinoa and add it to the saucepan. Cook the quinoa for twenty minutes or until it is tender and has absorbed the water.

3. Combine the eggs, Parmesan, quinoa, garlic, scallions, steamed spinach and breadcrumbs. Let the ingredients sit for some time to ensure that the flavors are absorbed.

4. Scoop the mixture and flatten them to form patties.

5. Place a non-stick skillet over medium heat and add oil to it. When the oil is hot, cook the patties on either side until they are golden.

6. Serve hot.

Spicy Seafood Stew

Total time: 30 minutes

Ingredients

- 5 fresh skinless fish fillets (any type)
- 6 ounces shrimp (washed, peeled and deveined)
- 2 tsp olive oil
- 1 cup onion (chopped)
- 1/2 cup carrot (Finely chopped)
- 1/2 cup red and green pepper (finely chopped)
- 2 cloves garlic (peeled, washed and minced)
- 1 bowl tomatoes (halved)
- 1 cup low-sodium tomato sauce
- 1 cup low-sodium chicken broth
- 1/4 cup red wine (alternatively, you can choose dry red wine)
- 2 bay leaves
- 1 tbsp fresh thyme (crushed)
- 1/2 tsp Cajun seasoning

- 1/4 tsp ground cumin

- 1/4 tsp red chili powder

Directions:

*1.*Thaw the fish, rinse and pat it dry. Cut the shrimp and transfer into a large dish. Add the fish to the bowl and cover the bowl until you need to use the shrimp and fish.

*2.*Place a large saucepan over medium heat and add olive oil to it. When the oil is warm, add onion and garlic to it. Stir the ingredients until the onion has turned golden brown and soft.

*3.*Now, add carrots and peppers to the pan and cook until the vegetables are soft. Add the halved tomatoes with their juice, wine, tomato sauce, chicken broth, bay leaves and dried thyme to the pan and stir. Cook until the vegetables are coated well with the tomato sauce.

*4.*Add Cajun seasoning, cumin powder and red chili powder to the pan. Stir the ingredients in the pan and bring them to a boil.

*5.*When the ingredients begin to boil lower the heat, cover the pan and continue to cook the ingredients for ten minutes.

*6.*Add the shrimp and fish to the pan and stir until the shrimp and fish are coated well with the sauce.

7.Cover the pan and cook for ten minutes. If the fish and shrimp are fully cooked, transfer the ingredients to a serving bowl.

8.Serve hot with brown rice.

Turkey and Vegetables Stir Fry

Total time: 20 minutes

Ingredients

- 2 tbsp olive oil
- 1/2 tsp salt
- 1 tsp ginger (minced)
- 2 cloves garlic (washed, peeled and minced)
- 2 cups turkey (cubed)
- 3 cups mixed vegetables (chopped)
- 1 tsp maple syrup
- 2 cups brown rice (cooked)

Directions:

1.Place a large skillet over medium heat and add oil to it. When the oil is warm, add ginger, garlic, vegetables, turkey and salt to the skillet and stir.

2. Cook until the turkey cubes turn brown.

3. Reduce the heat and add maple syrup to the skillet and continue to cook until the vegetables are tender.

4. Serve hot with brown rice.

Shepherd's Pie

Total time: 40 minutes

Ingredients

- 3 large potatoes (peeled, washed and diced)
- 1 cup low-fat milk
- 1-pound ground beef (preferably lean)
- 2 cups vegetable broth
- 2 cloves garlic (peeled, washed and minced)
- 2 tbsp flour
- 5 cups mixed vegetables (fresh or frozen)
- 1 cup cheddar cheese (shredded)
- 1 tsp ground pepper, to taste

Directions:

1. Place a pot on medium heat and add the diced potatoes to it. Cover the potatoes with enough water and cover the pot.

2. Bring the water to a boil and cook the potato until the pieces are soft.

3. Drain the water and mash the potatoes and add milk to the pot. Set this mixture aside.

4. Preheat the oven to 300 degrees Fahrenheit.

5. Place a skillet over medium heat and cook the onion, meat and garlic until the onions become soft and turn golden brown and the meat turns brown.

6. Add the broth and vegetables to the skillet and bring the ingredients to a boil.

Stir the ingredients well.

7. Line a baking dish with parchment paper and spoon the vegetable mixture into the dish. Transfer the potato mixture to the dish and sprinkle cheese on top.

8. Bake the ingredients for ten minutes or until the cheese has fully melted.

9. Serve hot.

Sweet Pepper Fish and Salsa

Total time: 30 minutes

Ingredients

- 1-pound fresh skinless fish fillets
- 1/2 tbsp olive oil
- 1 1/2 cups fresh mushrooms (washed, de-stemmed and quartered)
- 1 cup green and yellow peppers
- 1 small onion (peeled and finely sliced)
- 1 cup salsa

For Seasoning

- Oregano

Directions:

1. Thaw the fish and cut the fillets into smaller portions if you prefer.

2. Rinse the fish and pat it dry with the paper towels and set the fish aside.

3. Place a large skillet on medium heat and add one teaspoon of olive oil to it.

When the oil is warm, add the quartered mushrooms to the skillet.

4. Cook until the mushrooms have released their juices. Now, add the onion slices to the skillet and cook until the slices have turned golden brown and soft.

5. Now, add the green and yellow peppers to the skillet and stir until the vegetables are soft.

6. Transfer the vegetables to a plate and leave them to cool.

7. Place the same skillet over medium heat and add the remaining oil to it. When the oil is warm, add the fish fillets to the skillet and cook on both sides for ten minutes or until the fillets are lightly seared.

8. Add the salsa to the skillet and cover the skillet. Cook for ten minutes.

9. Uncover the skillet and transfer the vegetables from the plate to the skillet.

Stir the ingredients in the skillet until the vegetables are coated well with the salsa.

10. Garnish with the oregano and serve hot.

Pork Tenderloin with Sweet Potatoes and Apples

Total time: 47 minutes

Ingredients

- 1 cup apple cider
- 1/2 cup apple cider vinegar

- 3 tbsp maple syrup
- 1/2 tsp smoked paprika
- 2 tsp fresh ginger (grated)
- 1 tsp black pepper (ground)
- 3 tsp olive oil
- 1 12-ounce pork tenderloin
- 2 large sweet potatoes (cubed)
- 2 large apples (cored and cubed)

Directions:

*1.*Preheat the oven to 350 degrees Fahrenheit.

*2.*Combine the apple cider vinegar, apple cider, smoked paprika, ginger, maple syrup and black pepper. Set this mixture aside.

*3.*Place a Dutch oven over medium heat and add olive oil to it. When the oil is warm, add the pork tenderloin to the oven. Cook the pork for twelve minutes or until the pork is brown on all sides.

*4.*Add the sweet potato to the Dutch oven and pour the apple cider mixture over the potatoes and pork.

*5.*Cover the oven and cook for fifteen minutes. Roast the pork until the thermometer reads 150 degrees.

6. Turn the sweet potatoes in the oven and add the quartered apple around the pork.

7. Bake the ingredients for another ten minutes. Remove the pork, sweet potatoes and apple from the Dutch oven and let it cool to room temperature.

8. While the pork rests, let the cider mixture continue to cook in the oven. When it thickens, set it aside.

9. Slice the pork and transfer to a serving plate. Add the sweet potatoes and apple to the plate. Pour the cider reduction over the pork, sweet potatoes and apple and serve warm.

Stuffed Peppers

Total time: 22 minutes

Ingredients

- 6 large poblano peppers
- 1 cup brown rice (uncooked)
- 2 cups fresh grilled salsa
- 1 15 oz. can black beans
- 2 cups frozen corn
- 2 tsp cumin
- 2 tsp chili powder

- 1/4 tsp cayenne pepper
- 1 cup Mexican blend cheese (shredded)
- Ground black pepper, to taste

Directions:

1. Preheat the broiler.

2. Cook the brown rice and set aside. Follow the instructions on the package.

3. Slice the poblano peppers lengthwise and remove ribs and seeds.

4. Line a baking dish with parchment paper and place the peppers with their skin facing the top.

5. Broil the peppers for five minutes and flip them over. Broil for another five minutes. Ensure that the peppers do not burn and are slightly charred.

6. Drain the black beans and rinse them in cold water.

7. Combine the salsa, beans, corn, half a cup of cheese, cayenne pepper, chili powder and cumin in a microwave bowl and toss gently.

8. Heat the filling for three minutes in the microwave or until the filling is warm.

Stir every 30 seconds.

9. Add the rice to the bowl and toss until the filling is well combined.

10. Spoon the filling into the pepper and top with the remaining cheese.

11. Broil the peppers for another two minutes or until the cheese has fully melted.

12. Serve hot.

Thai Steak Salad

Total time: 2 hours 20 minutes

Ingredients

For the Salad

- 1-pound steak (preferably London broil)
- 2 tbsp soy sauce
- 1 1/2 tsp olive oil
- 1/2 clove garlic (peeled, washed and minced)
- 1/2 tsp ginger (grated)
- 5 ounces coleslaw mix
- 1 bunch green onions (sliced)
- 2 carrots (peeled, washed and sliced)

For the Dressing

- 1/4 cup white vinegar
- 1 1/2 tsp maple syrup
- 1 1/2 tsp vegetable oil
- 1/2 tbsp grated ginger
- 1/2 tsp salt

Directions:

1. Transfer the London broil steak into a plastic bag and add the garlic, soy sauce, ginger and olive oil in the proportions mentioned in the salad section of the ingredient list to it. Seal the bag and leave it in the refrigerator for two hours.

2. Heat a grill pan on high flame and place the steak over the pan and cook for at least six minutes. Turn the steak over and cook the other side for another six minutes.

3. Let the steak rest for some time.

4. Combine the coleslaw mix, carrots and onion in a large bowl.

5. In another small saucepan, combine all the dressing ingredients and place the pan over medium heat until the maple syrup has dissolved.

6. Add the warm dressing to the vegetables and set aside.

7. Cut the steak into thin slices and add to the salad and serve warm.

Thai Chicken Pasta Skillet Recipe

Total time: 30 minutes

Ingredients

- 6 oz. whole wheat spaghetti, uncooked
- 2 tsp. canola oil
- 1 package (10 oz.) sugar snap peas, cut into diagonal strips after trimming
- 2 cups (approximately 8 oz.) julienned carrots
- 2 cups shredded chicken, cooked
- 1 cup Thai peanut sauce
- 1 medium-sized cucumber, halved along the length, cut into diagonal strips
- Chopped cilantro for garnishing

Directions

1. In a vessel, boil the spaghetti until it is completely cooked. Drain the water and set aside the spaghetti.

2. While the spaghetti is cooking, in one large skillet, heat the canola oil, keeping the heat at a medium level. Add the snap peas along with the diced carrots.

3. Stir-fry the mixture for at least 6-8 minutes, maintaining the medium heat. When it turns crisp-tender, add the cooked shredded chicken, spaghetti, and peanut sauce. Keep the flame at a medium level to avoid overcooking. Also, keep tossing to combine the mixture properly and evenly.

4. Transfer the preparation to a flat serving plate. To make the dish more attractive, garnish with the sliced cucumber or cilantro.

Lentil Medley

Total time: 40 minutes

Ingredients

- 1 cup lentils, rinsed and dried
- 2 cups water
- 2 cups sliced mushrooms
- 1 medium-size cucumber, cut into cubes
- 1 medium-size zucchini, cut into cubes
- 1 chopped small red onion
- ½ cup chopped sun-dried tomato halves

- ½ cup rice vinegar
- ¼ cup minced mint
- 3 tbsp. olive oil
- 2 tsp. honey
- 1 tsp. dried basil
- 1 tsp. dried oregano
- 4 cups chopped fresh baby spinach
- 1 cup crushed feta cheese
- 4 bacon strips, crumbled and cooked

Directions

1. Place the lentils in a small saucepan. Add water to the saucepan. Bring it to a boil. Reduce the heat and let it simmer over low heat. Put a cover on the saucepan and let it sit for the next 20-25 minutes or until the lentils are tender. Once the lentils are cooked, drain the excess water and rinse under cold water.

2. Transfer the boiled lentils to a large bowl. Add the cucumber, mushrooms, zucchini, tomatoes, and onion. In a small bowl, whisk the vinegar with mint, honey, oil, basil, and oregano. Slowly drizzle over the lentil mixture and toss it to form a coat. You can also add cheese, spinach and, if required, bacon. Toss well to combine.

Spiced Salmon

Total time: 50 minutes

Ingredients

- 2 tbsp. brown sugar
- 4 tsp. chili powder
- 2 tsp. grated lemon zest
- ¾ tsp. ground cumin
- ½ tsp. salt
- ¼ tsp. ground cinnamon
- 4 salmon fillets (approximately 4 oz. each)

Directions

1. Combine the brown sugar, chili powder, lemon zest, ground cumin, salt, and cinnamon. Rub the spice mix over the salmon so that the spices evenly cover the surface of the fish. Set the marinated fish aside for a while so that the fish better absorbs the flavors.

2. Place the fillets in an 11x7-inch baking dish. Remember to coat the baking dish with cooking spray so that the fish does not stick to the surface during baking. Bake uncovered at 350° until the fish flakes easily with a fork. The usual time that this dish takes to be prepared is 15-20 minutes.

Tomato Green Bean Soup

Total time: 45 minutes

Ingredients

- 1 cup chopped onion

- 1 cup chopped carrots

- 2 tsp. butter

- 6 cups vegetable broth or reduced-sodium chicken

- 1 lb. fresh green beans, each cut into pieces measuring 1 inch

- 1 minced garlic clove

- 3 cups fresh tomatoes, diced properly

- ¼ cup minced basil or 1 tbsp. dried basil

- ½ tsp. salt

- ¼ tsp. pepper

Directions

1.Put a large saucepan over a flame and maintain medium heat throughout the preparation to keep the nutritional values of the vegetables intact. Sauté the onion and carrots in butter for 5 minutes while you toss the ingredients at regular intervals to avoid overcooking on any side.

2. Add the broth to the pan along with the beans and garlic. Bring the mixture to a boil. Reduce heat and cover the vessel. Let the mixture simmer for another 20 minutes or until the vegetables become tender.

3. Once the vegetables turn tender, stir in the basil, tomatoes, pepper, and salt. Cover the vessel once more and simmer for another 5 minutes.

4. Remove the saucepan from the flame and set the soup aside to settle. Pour it in a serving bowl and garnish with minced coriander leaves. Serve hot.

Citrus Herb Pot Roast

Total time: 5 hours 25 minutes

Ingredients

- Boneless pork of 3-4 lbs.
- 1 tsp. dried oregano
- ½ tsp. ground ginger
- ½ tsp. pepper
- 2 medium-sized onions, sliced into thin wedges
- 1 cup and 3 tbsp. orange juice, separated

- 1 tbsp. sugar
- 1 tbsp. white grapefruit juice
- 1 tbsp. steak sauce
- 1 tbsp. soy sauce with reduced-sodium
- 1 tsp. grated zest of orange
- ½ tsp. salt
- 3 tbsp. cornstarch
- Freshly prepared egg noodles
- Fresh oregano

Directions

1. Cut the roast into halves. Combine the ginger, oregano, and pepper and rub over the pork. In a large skillet coated with cooking spray, roast all sides until brown. Pour into a slow cooker and add onions.

2. Combine 1 cup orange juice, grapefruit juice, sugar, soy sauce, and steak sauce and pour over the top. Cook covered on low heat for 4-5 hours until tender. Place the meat and onions on a serving platter and keep warm.

3. Skim the fat from the cooking juices and transfer it to a saucepan. Add the salt and orange zest. Boil the mixture. Combine the cornstarch with orange juice until the mixture turns smooth. Stir gradually into the pan.

As it boils, stir and cook for 2 minutes until it thickens. Sprinkle fresh oregano and serve with pork and noodles.

Grilled Tilapia and Pineapple Salsa

Total time: 40 minutes

Ingredients

- 2 cups fresh pineapple, cut into cubes of even sizes
- 2 chopped green onions
- ¼ cup green pepper, finely chopped
- ¼ cup minced cilantro, fresh
- 4 tsp. and 2 tbsp. lime juice, separated
- ⅛ tsp. and ¼ tsp. salt, separated
- Dash cayenne pepper
- 1 tbsp. canola oil
- 8 pieces tilapia fillets (weighing around 4 oz. each)
- ⅛ tsp. pepper

Directions

1. For the salsa, in a small bowl, combine the pineapple, green pepper, green onions, cilantro, ⅛ tsp. salt, 4 tsp.

lime juice, and cayenne. Refrigerate the mixture until serving.

2. Mix the oil and the remaining lime juice and gradually drizzle over the fillets. Sprinkle the pepper and the remaining salt over the fillets as well.

3. Moisten a paper towel with cooking oil. Using long-handled forceps, rub it on the grill rack to make a light coating. Grill the fish as you keep it covered. Keep it over medium heat. Continue broiling from heat for 2-3 minutes on each of the sides or until the fish begins to flake with a fork. Once it starts flaking, the fish is ready to be served. You can now serve it hot with the salsa that you have kept in the refrigerator.

Mango Rice Pudding

Total time: 55 minutes

Ingredients

- 2 cups water
- ¼ tsp. salt
- 1 cup long-grain brown rice, uncooked
- 1 medium-sized ripe mango
- 1 cup soymilk or vanilla flavor
- 2 tbsp. sugar

- ½ tsp. ground cinnamon

- 1 tsp. vanilla extract

- Chopped mango, cleanly peeled

Directions

*1.*Pour water into a large, heavy saucepan. Add some salt to the water and place the saucepan on the oven, turning the flame on. Bring the water and salt to a boil. Gradually pour the rice into the boiling water, stirring gently to avoid clots. Turn the flame on low and, over medium heat, let the rice simmer. Put a cover over the saucepan and let cook for 35-40 minutes. Your rice is cooked when the water gets absorbed and the rice becomes tender.

*2.*When the rice is cooked, peel the mango and set the seed aside. Dice the mango pulp into cubes, then mash them with a fork or potato masher.

*3.*Mix the milk, cinnamon, sugar, and mashed mango with the rice. Remove the lid of the saucepan and cook over a low flame for 10-15 minutes. Wait until the liquid gets absorbed. Keep stirring occasionally.

*4.*Remove the pan from the heat and mix in the vanilla. Garnish with diced mango cubes and serve hot or cold.

Thai-Style Cobb Salad

Total time: 20 minutes

Ingredients

- 1 bunch of romaine, washed and torn
- 2 cups shredded rotisserie chicken
- 3 large eggs, hard-boiled and coarsely chopped
- 1 medium-sized ripe avocado, thinly sliced and neatly peeled
- 1 medium-sized carrot, neatly shredded
- 1 medium-size julienned sweet red pepper
- 1 cup fresh snow peas, each halved
- ½ cup unsalted peanuts
- ¼ cup fresh cilantro leaves
- ¾ cup salad Asian toasted sesame dressing
- 2 tbsp. smooth peanut butter

Directions

1. Place the romaine on a large serving platter. Arrange the chicken, coarsely chopped eggs, peeled and sliced avocado slices, and the rest of the vegetables and the peanuts and spread over the romaine. Mix the ingredients properly to distribute the components evenly.

2. Sprinkle some cilantro to add zest to this salad.

3. In a small bowl, whisk the salad dressing and the peanut butter to form a smooth mix. Your salad would be best served with this smooth mix of peanut butter and salad dressing.

Vegetable and Turkey Barley Soup

Total time: 30 minutes

Ingredients

- 1 tbsp. canola oil
- 5 medium-sized carrots, chopped
- 1 medium-sized onion, chopped
- 2/3 cup quick-cooking barley
- 6 cups chicken broth with reduced-sodium
- 2 cups turkey breast, cubed and cooked
- 2 cups baby spinach, fresh
- ½ tsp. pepper

Directions

1.Place a large saucepan over an oven and light the flame. Add oil to the pan and heat the oil over medium-high heat. Add the carrots and onion into the oil and cook for a while until the onion turns light brown. Keep stirring the mixture for 4-5 minutes until the carrots turn crisp-tender.

2.Once the vegetables are tender, pour the barley and the broth into the pan and bring the mixture to a boil.

3.After a while, reduce the heat and leave the mixture to simmer for 10-15 minutes with the saucepan covered with a lid. Check if the carrots and the barley have turned tender.

4.Once the vegetables are ready, add the turkey, pepper, and spinach. Cook for some more time for a perfect blend.

The dish is best served hot and contains a substantial amount of nutrients.

Grilled Steak Salad

Total time: 30 minutes

Ingredients

- ½ tsp. salt

- ½ tsp. garlic powder

- ½ tsp. pepper
- 1 lb. beef flank steak
- 1 sliced sweet onion, large
- 1 package spring mix salad greens
- 1 can kidney beans, washed and drained
- 1 jar roasted sweet red peppers, sliced and drained
- ⅓ cup balsamic vinegar
- 2 tsp. dried basil or 2 tbsp. minced fresh basil
- 2 tbsp. olive oil
- 1 tsp. Dijon mustard

Directions

*1.*Mix the salt, pepper, and garlic powder and rub over the steak. Grease the grill rack.

*2.*Grill the steak with a cover on, over medium heat for 6-8 minutes on each side until the meat is done.

*3.*Place the onion slices on heavy-duty foil of double thickness. Fold the foil around the onion and seal firmly. Grill over medium heat for 16-20 minutes until the onions are soft. Open the foil carefully and allow the vapor to escape.

4. Let the steak stand for another 5 minutes. Meanwhile, take a large bowl and mix the greens, red peppers, beans, and grilled onion.

5. In a small bowl, whisk the vinegar, oil, basil, and mustard. Transfer ¼ cup of vinegar mix over salad and toss to form a coat. Arrange the sliced flank steak over the salad and sprinkle the remaining dressing.

Garden Vegetable Beef Soup

Total time: 75 minutes

Ingredients

- 1 ½ lbs. ground beef
- 1 medium-sized onion, chopped
- 2 garlic cloves
- 10 oz. carrots, julienned
- 2 celery ribs, chopped
- ¼ cup tomato paste
- 1 can diced tomatoes
- 1 ½ cups cabbage, shredded
- 1 cup roughly chopped zucchini
- 1 finely chopped red potato

- ½ cup of chopped green beans
- 1 tbsp. dried basil
- ¼ tbsp. salt
- ¼ tbsp. pepper
- 1 tbsp. oregano
- 4 cans beef broth
- Parmesan cheese, grated

Directions

*1.*If you want to serve the dish to people of all ages, purchase low-sodium beef stock.

*2.*Put a deep pan on the oven and turn the heat to medium-high. Add the beef, chopped onions, and crushed garlic. Let the ingredients cook for about 8-9 minutes.

*3.*Add the celery and carrots. Stir these until the hard vegetable become soft. It will take another 6 minutes over medium-high heat.

*4.*Once the stock bubbles, add the tomato paste. Mix it well, along with the previous ingredients.

*5.*Add the chopped tomatoes, sweet potato, shredded cabbage, zucchini, and green beans, along with the beef broth.

6.Add the dry seasonings, salt, and pepper.

7.Turn the heat on medium-low and let the concoction simmer for 35-40 minutes.

8.Serve with sprinkled cheese on top of the veggie-beef soup.

Asparagus Soup

Total time: 30 minutes

Ingredients

- 2 sliced leeks
- 12 chopped green onions
- 3 tbsp. olive oil
- 2 tbsp. butter
- 2 ½ lbs. asparagus, roughly cut
- 4 cups chicken broth
- 1 cup cream
- ½ tbsp. salt
- ¼ tbsp. pepper

Directions

*1.*Place a pan on the oven. Turn on the fire to medium and add the olive oil, followed by the butter. Mix well until the butter melts completely.

*2.*Put in the sliced leeks and chopped onions. Sauté properly.

*3.*Add the chicken broth and the cut asparagus and stir well.

*4.*Cook this in the uncovered pan on low heat until the vegetables become soft.

*5.*Set aside some of the cooked asparagus garnishing while serving.

*6.*Pour the rest of the cooked broth and vegetable mixture into the blender and give it a few whisks. This will not only mix all the ingredients properly but will also change the texture into a thick liquid.

*7.*Place the pan on the heat again and pour in the smooth mixture.

*8.*Cook this for few minutes over very low heat. Add pepper, salt, and cream.

*9.*The last few stirs will make the soup ready to be served with cooked asparagus pieces.

Sweet Potato and Black Bean Rice Bowl

Total time: 30 minutes

Ingredients

- ¾ cup rice, long-grained
- ¼ tbsp. garlic salt
- 1 ½ cups water
- 4 tbsp. olive oil
- 1 diced sweet potato
- 1 chopped red onion
- 4 cups kale, chopped
- 1 can black beans
- 2 tbsp. chili sauce

Directions

1. First, cook the rice. To do this, place the required amounts of water, rice, and garlic salt into a rice cooker. Place it on the oven. Once it starts to boil, lower the heat and cook the rice for 15 minutes.

2. Use this time to cook the vegetables. Put some oil in a pan. Once the oil heats up, fry the diced sweet potatoes for 7 minutes.

3. To this, add the chopped onions. Cook for another 6 minutes. Add the kale. Finally, add the beans and cook some more.

4. Once the veggie/bean mixture is cooked, pour some olive oil and rice in the same pan.

5. After mixing the ingredients well, add some chili sauce and give it a final stir.

6. While serving, add some more sauce to the black bean/rice dish, according to your preference. This is only for those who like things extra spicy and hot.

Pesto Corn and Shrimp Salad

Total time: 30 minutes

Ingredients

- 4 medium-sized corn ears
- ½ cup fresh basil
- ¼ cup olive oil
- ½ tbsp. salt
- 1 ½ cups cherry tomatoes, diced in equal halves
- ⅛ tsp. pepper powder
- 1 medium ripe avocado

- 40 fresh shrimp

Directions

1. Put the ear of corn into boiling water. After about 5 minutes, the corn will become soft. Switch off the heat and set it aside to cool.

2. In a blender, put in some olive oil, salt, and basil leaves. Blend the ingredients properly.

3. Separate the corn kernels and place them in a container. Add diced cherry tomatoes, some salt, and pepper powder with avocado pulp and mix well. Pour the oil and basil mixture into the veggies. Toss together so that the flavored oil coats everything.

4. It is best to purchase de-threaded shrimp from the market to save time. Clean the shrimp and dry them at room temperature. Marinate with the basil oil and keep for some time.

5. Grill the shrimp for 4 minutes on each side.

6. In a big bowl, add the grilled shrimp and the vegetables. Mix these gently and serve in serving dishes.

Salmon with Pistachio Horseradish Crust

Total time: 30 minutes

Ingredients

- 6 fillets of salmon
- ⅓ cup sour cream
- 2/3 cup breadcrumbs
- 2/3 cup pistachios, chopped
- ½ cup shallots, chopped
- 3 tbsp. olive oil
- 2 tbsp. horseradish, prepared
- 1 tbsp. fresh dill
- ½ tbsp. orange or lemon zest
- ¼ tbsp. pepper flakes
- 1 minced clove of garlic

Directions

1. To prepare this amazing and satisfying nutritional dinner dish, you will need a microwave oven, as it will speed up the process.

2. Switch on the microwave and set it at 350 degrees.

3. Take a microwave-safe tray. Do not use any oil or grease on the tray. Simply place the salmon fillets on the tray so that the skin side is facing up.

4. Cover each fillet with an adequate amount of sour cream.

5. Put the minced garlic, pepper flakes, lemon zest, chopped shallots, chopped pistachios, and breadcrumbs in a separate bowl.

6. To this, add 3 tbsp. of olive oil. Then add the fresh dill.

7. Use the back of the spoon to lightly crush the ingredients. Once you are happy with the texture, mix all the ingredients well.

8. Coat the salmon fillets with the intensely flavored coating.

9. Place each fillet on the tray and put it in the oven for 15 minutes.

10. Remove the tray after 15 minutes to inspect whether the fish has been cooked.

11. While serving, drizzle some hot sauce on the fish to add more punch.

Shredded Pork Salad

Total time: 26 minutes

Ingredients

- 4 oz. boneless pork meat
- 1 ½ cups apple cider
- 1 cup green chilies, chopped

- 3 minced garlic cloves
- 1 ½ tbsp. salt
- 1 ½ tbsp. hot pepper sauce
- 1 tbsp. chili powder
- 1 tbsp. pepper
- 1 tbsp. cumin powder
- ½ tbsp. oregano flakes
- 12 cups salad greens, torn
- 1 can black beans
- 2 tomatoes, chopped
- 1 chopped red onion
- 1 cup corn
- 1 cup mozzarella or cotija cheese
- Any salad dressing

Directions

1. Get a pot big enough to cook the pork. To ensure infusion of flavors, set the heat at a low level.

2. In a separate bowl, add the seasoning ingredients. Add the apple cider, minced garlic, salt and pepper powder, hot pepper sauce, green chilies, and dried oregano. Mix these ingredients well and put it in the pot where you have been cooking the pork.

3. Turn the heat on low and let the pork cook for 6 to 8 hours. Once the time is up, separate the meat from the juices.

4. Place the green salad on the plate and put the cooked and shredded pork on it. Top the pork with the baked black beans.

5. Add the seasoned tomatoes, corn, onion, and cheese to the top of the pork to enhance the flavors.

White Wine Garlic Chicken

Total time: 30 minutes

Ingredients

- 4 boneless chicken breasts
- ½ lb. salt
- 2 tbsp. olive oil
- ¼ tbsp. pepper powder
- 2 cups baby corn, sliced
- 1 onion, chopped
- 2 garlic cloves, minced

- ½ cup white wine

Directions

1. Pound the boneless chicken so that it becomes soft. Make sure that the thickness of the breasts is not more than ½ inches; otherwise, you will have issues while cutting it.

2. Rub the pepper powder and salt into the chicken breasts to season them.

3. Put a heavy-bottom pan on a medium flame. Pour in the required amount of olive oil and heat it. Place the chicken breasts in the oil. Fry each side for no longer than 5 minutes.

4. In another pan, put a little bit of olive oil. Toss in the chopped onions and mushrooms. Fry these for 3 minutes. By this time, they will have formed a brown color and become soft.

5. Add the minced garlic pieces and stir the mixture for 30 seconds.

6. Pour in the wine and let the entire mixture boil gently. The wine will start to reduce after about 2 minutes.

7. Place the fried chicken breasts on the plate. Pour the wine blend over the chicken and serve. The flavors of the wine and the other ingredients will infuse into the chicken, making it more tender.

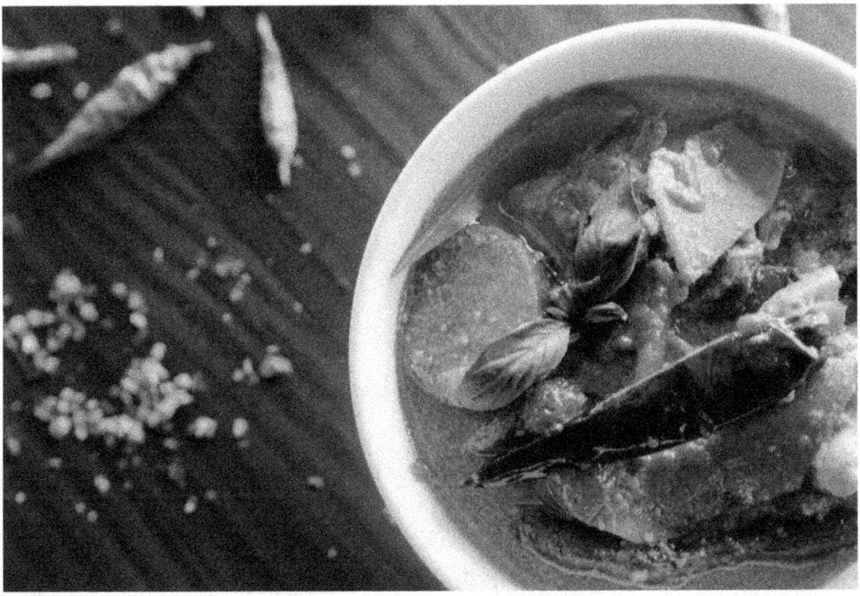

Chapter 13: Side Dish Dash Recipes

Overnight Oatmeal

Total time: 6 hours 15 minutes

Ingredients

- ½ cup oats
- 3 tbsp. milk, fat-free
- 3 tabs of low-fat yogurt
- 1 tbsp. fresh honey
- ½ cup assorted fruit
- 2 tbsp. roasted and chopped walnuts

Directions

If you have skipped breakfast or do not have time to prepare many things for lunch, this dish will keep you full for the rest of the day. It will also ensure that your nutritional requirements are met. Oatmeal is available in several flavors, but if you are old-fashioned, plain oatmeal will do just fine.

*1.*After opening the packet, measure ½ cup of oatmeal in a glass jar.

*2.*Pour in the milk.

3. Add the low-fat yogurt to the oatmeal and milk mixture.

4. With a long spoon, mix the 3 ingredients well.

5. Add the honey, which will add sweetness to the bland oats.

6. Give it another stir to ensure that everything has blended well.

7. Toss some walnuts in the microwave and roast them for some time. Then chop or slice them as per your preference. These will also go into the glass jar. You can use an assortment of chopped and diced fruit and berries.

8. Mix everything, and seal the jar tightly with a lid.

9. Keep it in the refrigerator for the entire night, and enjoy yummy overnight oatmeal in the morning.

Chili Lime Grilled Pineapple

Total time: 16 minutes

Ingredients

- 1 fresh medium pineapple
- 3 tbsp. brown sugar
- 1 tbsp. fresh lime juice

- 1 tbsp. olive oil
- 1 tbsp. fresh honey
- 2 tbsp. chili flakes
- Pinch of salt

Directions

If you are looking for an afternoon or evening snack, but want to stay on the path of healthy eating, this dish is ideal. It also takes less time to prepare.

1. Peel the pineapple. Remove the eyes and the outer skin to get to the inner fleshy and juicy part.

2. Cut the portions in the shape of long wedges. Carve out the entire pineapple in a similar manner

3. In a bowl, add the chili flakes and brown sugar. Crush these 2 ingredients a bit. Add a pinch of salt and honey. Pour in the lime juice and then stir the mixture lightly.

4. Coat the pineapple wedges with this mixture and let them sit for some time.

5. Once the liquids have penetrated the wedges, heat the grill.

6. Put these wedges on the hot grill. Keep each side on the flame for 4 minutes.

7. It is best to glaze these fruit wedges with the remaining mixture.

*8.*When the pineapple becomes brown, you'll know that the side is well-grilled and it is time for a flip.

Italian Sausage Stuffed Zucchini

Total time: 55 minutes

Ingredients

- 6 medium zucchinis
- 1 lb. Italian turkey sausage links with casings removed
- 2 seeded and chopped medium tomatoes
- 1 cup panko breadcrumbs
- ⅓ cup grated Parmesan cheese
- ⅓ cup minced fresh parsley
- 2 tbsp. minced fresh oregano
- 2 tbsp. minced fresh basil
- ¼ tsp. pepper
- ¾ cup shredded part-skim mozzarella cheese

Directions

*1.*Preheat the oven to 350°. Cut the zucchinis lengthwise in half and scoop out the pulp, while leaving

¼ inch of shell. Chop the pulp. Microwave the zucchinis until they turn crisp.

2. Cook the zucchini pulp and sausage in a skillet for 6 to 8 minutes over medium heat. When the sausage is no longer pink, break it into crumbles. After draining the mixture, stir in the tomatoes, Parmesan cheese, breadcrumbs, herbs, and pepper.

3. Spoon this mixture in the zucchini shells.

4. Place the shells into baking dishes and bake for 15 minutes (until the zucchini is tender). Sprinkle mozzarella cheese and bake for 5 minutes to let the cheese melt. Sprinkle minced parsley and serve.

Spicy Almonds

Total time: 50 minutes

Ingredients

- ⅓ cup brown sugar
- 2 tbsp. ground cumin
- 1 tbsp. ground coriander and ground cinnamon
- ½ tsp. ground ginger and smoked paprika
- ¼ tsp. cayenne pepper
- 1-2 tsp. kosher salt

- ½ tsp. freshly ground black pepper
- 1 egg white
- About 3 cups raw almonds

Directions

1. Preheat the oven to 300°F. Use a parchment paper to line a rimmed baking sheet.

2. Stir the brown sugar, salt, spices, and pepper into a medium bowl.

3. Put the egg white in another medium bowl and whisk for about 30 seconds (until it turns frothy). Add the almonds and toss it around with a spoon until the almonds are completely coated. Add the spice mixture and toss it until the nuts are evenly coated.

4. Spread the mixture evenly on the baking sheet.

5. Place the sheet in the oven and bake until toasted and fragmented. Stir it once. Cook for at least 45 minutes.

6. Let it cool completely and then serve it.

7. You can keep the nuts in a jar or a sealed bag at room temperature for several days.

Cannellini Bean Hummus

Total time: 20 minutes

Ingredients

- 1 can drained and rinsed cannellini beans (15 oz.)
- 2 tbsp. extra virgin olive oil
- 2 heaping tbsp. tahini
- 1 minced clove garlic
- Juice of 2 lemons
- ½ tsp. onion powder, optional
- Couple twists of the Himalayan salt grinder
- 2 tbsp. water as needed to thin

Directions

This recipe has a fun twist and offers a good result.

1. First, blend all the ingredients (other than the water) in a food processor until you reach the desired consistency.

2. Taste the end product to see if you need to add anything else. Often, a bit more salt or lemon will make the hummus tastier. Once you add the extra ingredients, blend again. Add 1 tbsp. of water whenever needed for thinning.

*3.*Serve it at room temperature or chilled. To garnish, use coriander or cumin leaves. Even zaatar looks nice as a topper.

*4.*Once garnished, plate it and enjoy it with your fries.

Portobello Mushrooms Florentine

Total time: 40 minutes

Ingredients

- 8 large stemmed portobello mushrooms
- 1 ½ lbs. fresh baby spinach
- 1 tbsp. olive oil
- 2 tbsp. unsalted butter
- 1 tbsp. fresh lemon juice
- 1 tbsp. whole-wheat pastry flour
- 3 oz. shredded provolone
- ¾ cup whole milk
- 8 medium eggs
- ½ tsp. lemon zest
- 1 tbsp. toasted pine nuts

Directions

1.Preheat the oven to 200° while simultaneously heating a grill pan over medium-high heat.

2.Brush oil onto the mushroom tops and grill until it is softened and charred. It takes about 5 minutes on each side.

3.Transfer it to the oven and keep warm.

4.In a large pot, cook the spinach over medium heat until it wilts. After 3-5 minutes, drain it and add lemon juice, butter, and salt. Drain again.

5.In the meantime, melt 1 tbsp. of butter over medium heat and add flour. Whisk the flour for 1 minute until it is golden.

6.Add the milk and whisk it until it thickens. This takes about 3 minutes. Once this is done, add the cheese and whisk until it smoothens.

7.Boil 3 inches of water in a large skillet at reduced heat. Poach the egg white and add it to the mushrooms. Plate it with lemon zest, pine nuts, and pepper. Serve hot.

Asparagus and Horseradish Dip

Total time: 30 minutes

Ingredients

- 2 lbs. fresh asparagus
- 2 tbsp. prepared horseradish
- 1 cup mayonnaise
- 1 tbsp. Dijon mustard
- 2 tbsp. minced flat-leaf parsley

Directions

1. Blanch the asparagus in boiling saltwater. Soak it for about a minute.

2. While removing the spears, rinse them under cold water to stop the cooking. After removing all the spears, pat it dry and leave it to dry correctly.

3. Mix the horseradish, mustard, mayonnaise, and parsley in a small bowl and whisk until it is well blended. Once mixed properly, add the asparagus to it.

4. Your dish is ready. It tastes best when served cold, so store it in a refrigerator until further use.

Peppered Tuna Kebabs

Total time: 55 minutes

Ingredients

- ½ cup thawed frozen corn

- 4 chopped green onions
- 1 chopped and seeded jalapeno pepper
- 2 tbsp. lime juice
- 2 tbsp. coarsely chopped fresh parsley
- 1 tsp. coarsely ground pepper
- 1 lb. of tuna steaks, cut into 1-inch cubes
- 1 medium peeled mango, cut into 1-inch cubes
- 2 large sweet red peppers

Directions

1. Set aside 5 ingredients in a small bowl for salsa.

2. Rub the tuna with pepper. An efficient way to do this is by taking soaked wooden skewers and alternately threading tuna, mango, and red peppers.

3. After that step, half of the preparation is done. Now, place the skewers on the greased grill rack and cook them.

4. To cook them, cover and let them cook at medium heat. Turn at regular intervals for a well-distributed cook.

5. It takes about 10 to 12 minutes for the tuna to turn pink in the center (medium-rare) and for the peppers to turn tender. Once this is done, serve hot with the salsa you made.

Grapefruit, Mint, and Lime Yogurt Parfait

Total time: 40 minutes

Ingredients

- 4 cups reduced-fat plain yogurt
- 3 tbsp. honey
- 2 tbsp. lime juice
- Torn fresh mint leaves
- 2 tsp. grated lime zest
- 4 large red grapefruit

Directions

*1.*The cutting of the grapefruit is the most important part of the preparation. You must cut the fruit into thin slices. Then remove the cover of the fruit from the pulp. Also, remove any other membrane of the fruit, which is not good to taste.

*2.*Mix the yogurt with lime zest and lime juice. This will add a great flavor to the yogurt.

*3.*Put the yogurt and grapefruit layers in parfait glasses to create a layered dish.

4.Store in the refrigerator for at least 10 minutes before serving. This is best served cold; the cooler, the better.

5.Chop a few fresh mint leaves. These will add a zing of freshness to the dish.

6.You can also add honey on the top, like a condiment. It tastes amazing with honey or lime juice on top.

Layered Hummus Dip

Total time: 45 minutes

Ingredients

- 1 carton (10 oz.) hummus
- 1 large English cucumber, chopped
- ½ cup Greek olives, chopped
- ¼ cup finely chopped red onion
- 1 cup crumbled feta cheese
- 2 medium tomatoes, seeded and chopped
- Baked pita chips

Directions

1.Spread the hummus into an at-least-10-inch round dish. Make sure all parts of the dish are covered with hummus.

2.Chop the onions, cucumber, tomatoes, olives, and cheese. It is best to chop them into small cubes.

3.When the dip is done, refrigerate it until you serve the dish.

4.Serve the food with any kind of chips, which will add to the taste.

Fruit and Almond Bites

Total time: 2 hours 20 minutes

Ingredients

- 3 ¾ cups divided and sliced almonds
- ¼ cup honey
- ¼ tsp. almond extract
- 2 cups finely chopped and dried apricots
- 1 cup toasted and finely chopped pistachios
- 1 cup finely dried and chopped cherries or cranberries

Directions

1.Take a little more than 1 cup of almonds and put it in a food processor. Chop the almonds into fine pieces and then keep them for coating purposes.

2. Put the rest of the almonds into the food processor. Finely chop them as well.

3. Add the extract to the almonds. Also add the honey when you are processing the almonds. Put the mixture in a large bowl and add the apricots and cherries. Divide into six portions and shape each one into ½-inch rolls.

4. Refrigerate the rolls for about an hour until they are firm.

5. Cut the rolls into small pieces and then roll some of them in the reserved almonds. The rest of them can be rolled in pistachios.

6. Wrap them in wax paper and store in an airtight container.

Quinoa Veggie Dip

Total time: 35 minutes

Ingredients

- 15 oz. rinsed and drained black beans
- 1 ½ tsp. ground cumin and paprika
- ½ tsp. cayenne pepper
- 1 2/3 cups water
- Salt and pepper to taste

- 2/3 cup rinsed quinoa

- 5 tbsp. lime juice

- 2 peeled and coarsely chopped medium ripe avocados

- 2 tbsp. and ¾ cup sour cream

- ¼ cup minced fresh cilantro

- 3 chopped tomatoes

- ¾ cup zucchini and peeled, seeded, and finely chopped cucumber

- ¼ cup finely chopped red onion

- Cucumber slices

Directions

1. Put the cumin, beans, paprika, cayenne pepper, and ⅓ cup water into a food processor and blend until smooth. Add pepper and salt for taste.

2. Cook the quinoa with water in a small saucepan, according to the directions in the package. Fluff it up with a fork and add 2 tbsp. lime juice. Set it aside.

3. Mash together the cilantro, avocados, 2 tbsp. sour cream, and rest of the lime juice in a bowl.

4. In a dish, layer the bean mix, quinoa, and avocado mix, rest of the sour cream, chopped cucumber, tomatoes, zucchini, and onion. Put cucumber slices on top and serve immediately or refrigerate.

Almond Chai Granola

Total time: 1 hour 40 minutes

Ingredients

- 2 tea bags
- ¼ cup boiling water
- 3 cups quick-cooking oats
- 2 cups coarsely chopped almonds,
- 1 cup sweetened coconut, shredded
- ½ cup honey
- ¼ cup olive oil
- ⅓ cup sugar
- 2 tsp. vanilla extract
- ¾ tsp. salt
- ¾ tsp. ground cinnamon
- ¾ tsp. ground nutmeg
- ¼ tsp. ground cardamom

Directions

1. Preheat the oven to 250°.

2. Dip the tea bags inside the boiling water and keep them there for 5 minutes

3. Combine the almond, oats, and coconut

4. Throw away the tea bag

5. Stir well the leftover ingredients of the tea.

6. Pour the tea mixture on the oat mixture and then mix well for a thick coating

7. Spread the coated oats over a greased rimmed pan.

8. Keep baking until the mixture appears to be golden brown while stirring it continuously every 20 minutes. Bake it for around 1 ¼ hours

9. Cease stirring. Let the entire mixture cool down

10. Store in an airtight container

Chickpea Mint Tabbouleh

Total time: 30 minutes

Ingredients

- 1 cup bulgur

- 2 cups water
- 1 cup thawed fresh peas (about 5 oz.)
- 1 can/15 ounce rinsed and drained garbanzo beans or chickpeas
- ½ cup minced fresh parsley
- ¼ cup minced fresh mint
- ¼ cup olive oil
- 2 tbsp. julienned sun-dried tomatoes, soft; make sure they are not packed in oil
- 2 tbsp. lemon juice
- ½ tsp. salt
- ¼ tsp. pepper

Directions

1. Add water to a large saucepan.

2. Put all the bulgur inside the saucepan and bring the mixture to a boil.

3. Reduce the heat just below the boiling level and keep covered for around 10 minutes.

4. Add the fresh peas and cook for some time. Keep it covered for 5 minutes until the peas get tender.

5.Transfer the whole mixture into a large bowl and keep stirring so that all the remaining ingredients are well mixed.

6.You can serve the Chickpea Mint Tabbouleh warm, or you can refrigerate it and serve it cold.

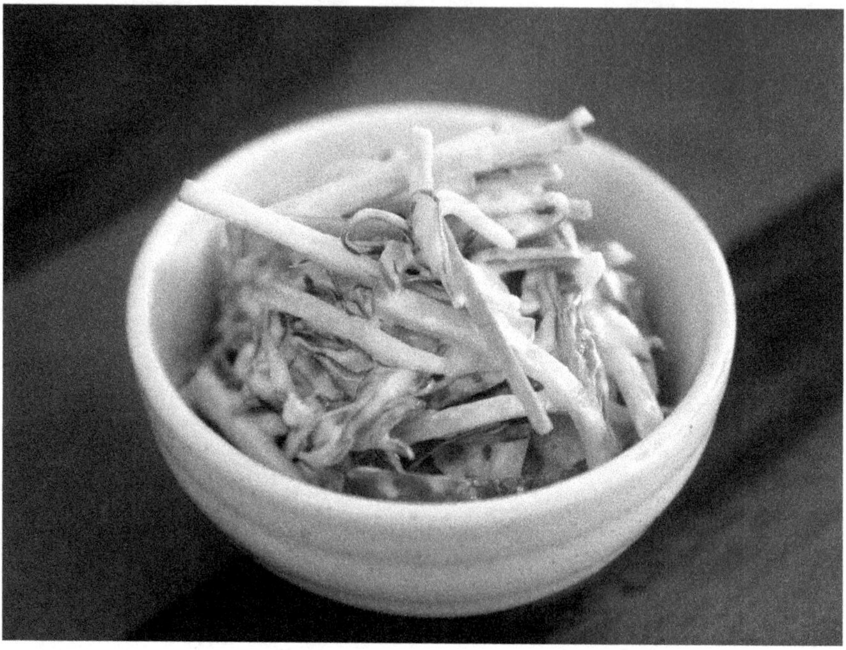

Chapter 14: Other Dash Recipes

Portobello mushrooms with ricotta, tomato, and mozzarella

Total time: 25 minutes

Ingredients

- 6 portobello mushroom caps, stemmed, gills removed
- 1 tablespoon extra-virgin olive oil
- 1 ½ cups part-skim ricotta, divided
- 3 small Roma tomatoes, thinly sliced
- ¾ cup shredded part-skim mozzarella cheese

Directions

1. Preheat the oven to 400°F. Line a baking sheet with parchment paper or aluminum foil.

2. Clean any debris from the outer mushroom caps with a damp paper towel. Rub the inner and outer portions of the mushroom caps with olive oil and place them, top-side down, on the prepared baking sheet.

3. Spread ¼ cup of ricotta over the inside of each mushroom cap. Top each mushroom cap with tomato slices and sprinkle with about 1 tablespoon of mozzarella cheese.

4. Bake for 15 to 20 minutes, or until the cheese turns golden brown. Serve immediately.

Pinto bean–stuffed sweet potatoes

Total time: 1 hour 20 minutes

Ingredients

- 6 medium sweet potatoes, scrubbed and patted dry

- 1 (16-ounce) can low-sodium pinto beans, rinsed well and drained

- 3 medium tomatoes, seeded and diced

- 1 tablespoon extra-virgin olive oil

- 1 ½ teaspoons ground cumin

- 1 ½ teaspoons ground coriander

- ⅛ teaspoon kosher salt

- 1 cup low-fat plain Greek yogurt, divided

Directions

1. Preheat the oven to 400°F. Line a rimmed baking sheet with aluminum foil.

2. Using a fork, prick the outside of each sweet potato in about 5 or 6 different places. Place the sweet potatoes on the prepared baking sheet and bake for about 45 minutes to 1 hour, depending on size. Remove from the oven and set aside.

3. In a small saucepan over medium heat, combine the pinto beans, tomatoes, olive oil, cumin, coriander, and salt. Cook for 3 to 4 minutes until warm, then remove from the heat.

4. When the sweet potatoes are cool enough to handle, halve each sweet potato lengthwise. Using a metal spoon, gently press down on the flesh of the potato, creating a small well. Fill the well with the bean-tomato mixture and top each with about 2 tablespoons of yogurt.

Roasted vegetables

Total time: 30 minutes

Ingredients

- Nonstick cooking spray, for preparing the baking sheet

- 2 tablespoons extra-virgin olive oil

- 4 garlic cloves, minced

- ½ teaspoon Salt-Free Italian Seasoning

- 2 cups fresh broccoli florets

- 1 zucchini, cut into 1-inch coins

- 1 yellow squash, sliced and quartered
- 1 red bell pepper, membranes removed, cut into ½-inch strips
- 1 medium red onion, quartered
- Kosher salt
- Freshly ground black pepper

Directions

1. Coat a rimmed baking sheet with cooking spray after preheating at 420°F. Set aside.

2. In a large bowl, whisk together the olive oil, garlic, and Italian seasoning.

3. Add the broccoli, zucchini, yellow squash, red bell pepper, and red onion. Gently toss to coat.

4. Spread the vegetable mixture on the prepared baking sheet. Roast for 13 to 16 minutes, or until tender. Season with salt and pepper.

Green beans with toasted almonds

Total time: 20 minutes

Ingredients

- 1 ½ pounds fresh green beans, trimmed

- 2 tablespoons extra-virgin olive oil
- 2 teaspoons butter
- ½ cup slivered almonds
- 1 garlic clove, minced
- 2 tablespoons freshly squeezed lemon juice
- Kosher salt
- Freshly ground black pepper

Directions

1. Fill a 6-quart pot with 2 inches of water and bring it to a boil over high heat. Add the green beans and boil for 2 minutes, or until crisp-tender. In a large colander, drain and rinse the green beans under cold running water until completely cool. Place the green beans on a clean kitchen towel and gently pat.

2. In a large skillet, heat the olive oil and butter over medium-low heat until the butter melts and the foam subsides.

3. Stir in the almonds and toast for about 3 minutes, stirring occasionally, until they're golden brown, making sure they do not burn. Using a slotted spoon or metal spatula, transfer the almonds to a plate to cool.

4. Decrease the heat under the skillet to low and add the garlic. Cook, stirring constantly, for 1 minute.

Increase the heat to medium and add the green beans. Cook for 4 to 7 minutes, tossing frequently, until the green beans become lightly browned in places.

*5.*Add the lemon juice and toss to mix. Season with salt and pepper. Transfer to a serving dish and sprinkle with the toasted almonds.

Balsamic berries and ricotta

Total time: 10 minutes

Ingredients

- ¼ cup balsamic vinegar
- 1 tablespoon loosely packed brown sugar
- 1 teaspoon vanilla extract
- ½ cup fresh strawberries, sliced
- ½ cup fresh raspberries
- ½ cup fresh blackberries
- ½ cup part-skim ricotta

Directions

*1.*In a medium bowl, whisk the vinegar, brown sugar, and vanilla until well combined.

2.Add the strawberries, raspberries, and blackberries. Gently toss to coat. Marinate the fruit for 15 minutes. Drain and discard the marinade.

3.To serve, divide the ricotta between two small dishes and top each with half the berry mixture.

Oatmeal dark chocolate chip peanut butter cookies

Total time: 25 minutes

Ingredients

- 1 ½ cups natural creamy peanut butter
- ½ cup packed dark brown sugar
- ½ teaspoon kosher salt
- 2 large eggs
- 1 cup old-fashioned rolled oats
- 1 teaspoon baking soda
- ½ cup dark chocolate chips

Directions

1. Line a baking sheet with parchment paper after preheating. Set aside.

2. In the bowl of a stand mixer fitted with the paddle attachment, whip the peanut butter until very smooth.

3. Continue beating and add the brown sugar, mixing until combined.

4. One at a time, add the eggs, beating the first one until fluffy before adding the next.

5. Mix in the oats, baking soda, and salt until combined.

6. Using a rubber spatula, fold in the chocolate chips by hand.

7. Using a small cookie scoop or teaspoon, place small portions of cookie dough on the prepared baking sheet about 2 inches apart. Bake for 8 to 10 minutes, depending on your preferred level of doneness.

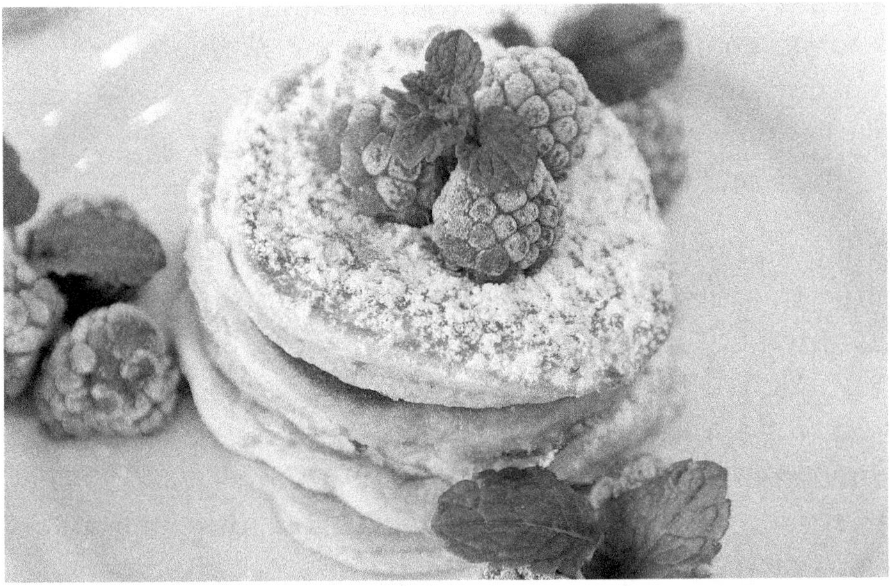

CONCLUSION

Perhaps you were interested in this book because you were guided to the DASH Diet under a physician's advice, or maybe you had just heard that the DASH Diet was once again rated among the top diet plans out there today and you decided it was finally time to make positive changes in your life and health. Whatever your reasons, or your path, here you are and now you have all the information you need to get you through the first 14 days on the DASH Diet plan effortlessly.

While you are certain to notice positive health benefits after this first 30 days, now is the time to make the commitment to yourself to keep going, to start living the DASH lifestyle now and in the future. Fresh, flavorful and healthy are the concepts to keep in mind when creating your DASH eating plan. You will find that when you stick to these concepts, that delicious meals just fall together without much time or effort on your part.

Use what you have learned here and apply it not only to your life, but to those that you care about as well. Show them just how important taking care of their health is, and how very simple it can actually be. Best wishes on your new path to health as you go forward with your DASH Diet lifestyle.

CPSIA information can be obtained
at www.ICGtesting.com
Printed in the USA
BVHW051715240123
656999BV00022B/495

9 798613 468164